OECD ECONOMIC SURVEYS

1993-1994

ICELAND

ORGANISATION FOR ECONOMIC CO-OPERATION AND DEVELOPMENT

ORGANISATION FOR ECONOMIC CO-OPERATION AND DEVELOPMENT

Pursuant to Article 1 of the Convention signed in Paris on 14th December 1960, and which came into force on 30th September 1961, the Organisation for Economic Co-operation and Development (OECD) shall promote policies designed:

— to achieve the highest sustainable economic growth and employment and a rising standard of living in Member countries, while maintaining financial stability, and thus to contribute to the development of the world economy;
— to contribute to sound economic expansion in Member as well as non-member countries in the process of economic development; and
— to contribute to the expansion of world trade on a multilateral, non-discriminatory basis in accordance with international obligations.

The original Member countries of the OECD are Austria, Belgium, Canada, Denmark, France, Germany, Greece, Iceland, Ireland, Italy, Luxembourg, the Netherlands, Norway, Portugal, Spain, Sweden, Switzerland, Turkey, the United Kingdom and the United States. The following countries became Members subsequently through accession at the dates indicated hereafter: Japan (28th April 1964), Finland (28th January 1969), Australia (7th June 1971) and New Zealand (29th May 1973). The Commission of the European Communities takes part in the work of the OECD (Article 13 of the OECD Convention).

3 2280 00497 9795

Publié également en français.

Table of contents

3

Tables

Diagrams

Text

BASIC STATISTICS OF ICELAND

THE LAND

Area (1 000 sq. km)	103	Unproductive area (1 000 sq. km)	82
Productive area (1 000 sq. km)	21	*of which:*	
of which:		Glaciers	12
Cultivated area	1.1	Other area devoid of vegetation	70
Rough grazings	20		

THE PEOPLE

Population, 1st December 1993	264 922	Occupational distribution, 1991 (per cent):	
Net increase 1982-92, annual average		Agriculture	5.4
(per cent)	1.1	Fishing and fish processing	11.5
		Other manufacturing	12.5
		Construction, total	9.8
		Commerce	14.6
		Communications	6.9
		Services and other	39.3
			100.0

GOVERNMENT AND PARLIAMENT

	1987	1991
Parliament, number of seats:		
Independence Party (Lib. Cons.)	18	26
Progressive Party (Agrarians)	13	13
Peoples' Alliance (Socialists, Communists)	8	9
Social Democratic Party	10	10
Citizen's Party	7	–
Women's Alliance	6	5
Other	1	–
	63	63

Last general election: April 1992

PRODUCTION AND CAPITAL FORMATION

Gross national product in 1993:		Gross fixed capital formation in 1993:	
IKr million	382 996	IKr million	61 300
Per head, US dollars	21 386	Per cent of GNP	16.0

FOREIGN TRADE

Exports of goods and services in 1993,		Imports of goods and services in 1993,	
per cent of GNP	35.8	per cent of GNP	32.0
Main exports in 1993 (per cent of		Imports in 1993, by use (per cent of	
merchandise exports):		merchandise imports):	
Fish products	78.7	Consumer goods	33.1
Aluminium	8.7	Investment goods	29.9
Other manufacturing products	8.9	Intermediate goods (excl. fuels)	28.0
Agricultural products	1.7	Fuels and lubricants	9.0
Miscellaneous	2.0		

THE CURRENCY

Monetary unit: Krona		Currency units per US dollar,	
		averages of daily figures:	
		Year 1993	67.6
		February 1994	73.1

Note: An international comparison of certain basic statistics is given in an annex table.

This Survey is based on the Secretariat's study prepared for the annual review of Iceland by the Economic and Development Review Committee on 7th March 1994.

•

After revisions in the light of discussions during the review, final approval of the Survey for publication was given by the Committee on 31st March 1994.

•

The previous Survey of Iceland was issued in May 1993.

Introduction

Iceland had to endure another year of economic stagnation in 1993. Although output probably crept up marginally in real terms, incomes fell significantly because of severe weakness in the terms of trade, largely the result of substantial declines in world prices for its all-important marine exports. The labour market remained weak, although the unemployment rate seemed to have stabilised in the 5 per cent range. The 1993 outcome was not, however, as dismal as had been expected. The fish catch was larger than had been anticipated due to greater recourse to waters beyond Iceland's economic zone, an increase in yield from fishing methods not subject to catch quotas and a larger take of certain species, especially capelin, whose stocks are in better shape than those of cod. Furthermore, despite another devaluation of the krona in June, inflation remained modest and by year-end showed signs of returning to the near-zero rates recorded through most of 1992. In May 1993 national wage agreements implied unchanged wages until the end of 1994. Languishing domestic demand led to sharply curtailed imports and, combined with increased export earnings, a tiny surplus on the current account for the first time since 1986.

From a policy point of view, the year 1993 was marked by several features. The severity of the income deterioration, combined with the need to impose a further enormous reduction in the total allowable catch for cod, forced the second devaluation within a year. Also, fiscal slippage, largely the product of concessions deemed necessary to bring about the wage freeze, resulted in a Treasury deficit well above the targeted level. But the authorities managed to achieve a considerable reduction in nominal and real rates of interest toward the end of 1993, without pressures on the exchange rate, allowing greater confidence that once cod catches stabilise, the economy will begin to recover. And the groundwork for the medium term was laid with the entry into force this year of the

European Economic Area agreement and all the structural reforms that has required.

This Survey begins with a chapter describing recent economic outcomes in more detail, before moving on to a close examination of the policy stance in Chapter II. That chapter starts with a review of recent budgetary outcomes and then presents the main lines of the budget for 1994. It also explains the authorities' monetary and exchange-rate objectives, and what they were able to achieve. Finally, it surveys the structural reforms that have been undertaken in financial markets and other domains. Chapter III focuses on problems in the agricultural sector, scrutinises the state of Iceland's environment, as well as the associated policies that have been proposed or implemented, and then probes the fisheries management situation. Lastly, conclusions are drawn in Chapter IV.

I. Recent trends and projections

Developments in 1993

Over the past six years, the troubles of Iceland's fishing sector, along with the more recent world-wide recession, have caused the economy to stagnate. Low stocks of cod have forced cut-backs in the catch, driving down overall export revenues and national income. Income losses were compounded by a 22 per cent decline in average world fish prices (in SDR terms) between January 1992 and September 1993. However, the fisheries showed remarkable resilience last year, finding new sources of revenue. The overall fish catch actually increased, contributing to a 1 per cent rise in real GDP (Diagram 1). Even so, weak fish prices led to a decline in real national income, and output outside the fisheries was hurt by the resulting drop in domestic demand. Sluggish activity held down price inflation to about 4 per cent, despite the devaluations of November 1992 and June 1993.

In 1993 water temperature and plankton levels around Iceland were favourable for growth of the fish stock. This was the third straight year of good environmental conditions, and for the first time since 1984 the stock of newly hatched cod picked up significantly. However, these fish will not be big enough to catch until late in the decade, and several years of such favourable spawnings are needed to get the cod fisheries onto a sustainable long-run path. In the meantime, the fishable stock of mature cod is close to the lowest on record, and thus for the 1993/94 fisheries year the government was once more forced to cut cod quotas[1]. However, quotas for capelin were increased sharply for the past two fisheries years, offsetting some of the lost revenues from cutbacks in the cod catch. Another important development for the fisheries in 1993 was the shift of many boats out of Iceland's traditional coastal fishing grounds into new regions, including the Barents Sea, the Flemish Hat off the coast of Newfoundland and

11

Diagram 1. **AGGREGATE ECONOMIC PERFORMANCE**

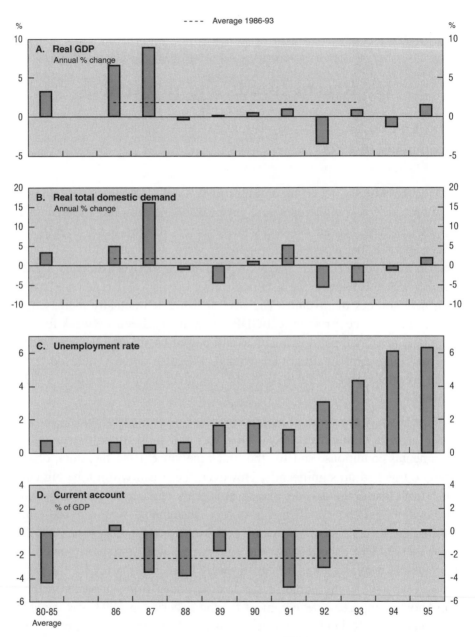

Source: National Economic Institute; OECD, *National Accounts* and OECD projections.

deep-sea areas beyond Iceland's fishing zone. Thus, the overall real catch may have increased about 4 per cent in 1993[2], ending a string of five straight years of output declines in the sector (Diagram 2).

While fisheries output increased in 1993, fisheries revenues were not nearly as favourable. Weak world demand and increased competition from Eastern Europe drove down world fish prices until September (Diagram 3). Even with a limited recovery in fish prices in the fourth quarter of 1993, overall export revenues of the fisheries were well below 1992 levels: as a rule, only the most efficient freezer trawlers avoided losses for the year[3]. In January of this year, the fishermen's union alleged that some fishing firms were requiring employees to participate financially in purchasing quotas, in contravention of their labour contract, and that profits were being artificially lowered by means of transfer price manipulation in order to reduce profit-sharing payments – practices that resulted in a two-week strike starting the first of the year[4]. Fortunately for all concerned in the fisheries sector, profitability improved somewhat in early 1994, with higher fish prices and the establishment of the European Economic Area. As

Diagram 2. **THE FISH CATCH**

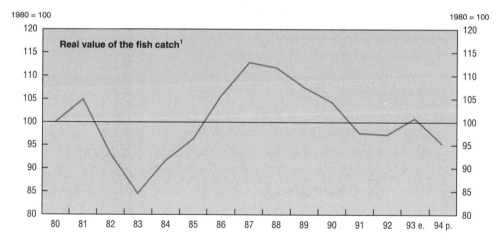

Note: e = estimate; p = projection.
1. Includes catch of fish in foreign waters. Catch volumes of each species are weighted using domestic fish prices of 1990.
Source: National Economic Institute.

Diagram 3. **EXPORT PRICES AND THE TERMS OF TRADE**

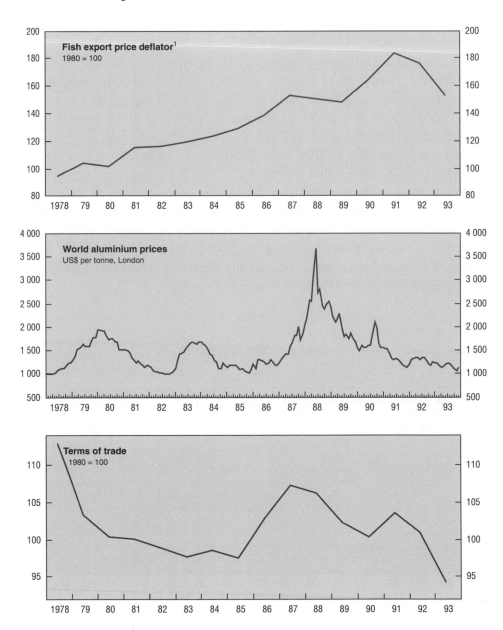

1. Trade-weighted foreign-currency export price index.
Source: Central Bank of Iceland, National Economic Institute, OECD.

a result of EEA implementation, EC tariffs on imported fish fell by about 76 per cent in January (2¼ percentage points of the 1990 price): ultimately tariffs on EC fish imports from Iceland will fall by a total of 90 per cent.

Other export sectors were not able to provide a significant boost to national income in 1993: as a rule production rose in these sectors (Table 1), but often revenues did not. For example, aluminium prices continued to fall, with recession-related weakness in world demand and increased competition from producers in the former Soviet Union (FSU)[5] – but Icelandic production levels rose slightly. Eastern Europe and China provided greater competition in ferro-silicon production than in the past, but capacity utilisation increased in 1993 in Iceland's plant nonetheless. Tourism picked up sharply. However, NATO budget cuts led

Table 1. **Export production, foreign trade and the current account**

Volume changes on previous year, per cent

	1987	1988	1989	1990	1991	1992	1993[1]
Export production							
Marine products	4.9	−0.2	−2.3	−1.2	−2.6	−2.0	6.0
Aluminium	9.7	−1.7	7.8	−1.8	2.7	0.4	1.5
Ferrosilicon	−18.3	14.7	3.8	−12.2	−20.6	8.7	27.5
Other goods	44.0	−1.8	13.5	−0.8	−16.0	−10.5	−1.4
Total	8.3	−0.3	1.8	−1.8	−3.8	−2.6	6.7
Merchandise exports, total	4.4	−1.2	3.5	−1.4	−7.9	−1.0	5.1
Merchandise imports, total	25.0	−5.5	−10.9	0.3	4.9	−7.6	−14.1
General merchandise imports	23.7	−8.1	−12.1	−0.5	4.9	−7.4	−7.0
Thereof:							
Oil imports	8.0	−1.7	14.8	0.4	−15.5	11.8	−3.5
Other imports	25.2	−8.6	−14.3	−0.6	10.5	−11.3	−9.2
Special imports[2]	34.0	13.6	−2.4	8.3	−12.0	−0.1	−37.2
Exports of non-factor services	2.2	−9.3	−0.1	3.7	−0.3	−3.7	8.6
Imports of non-factor services	18.0	−1.8	−8.3	3.0	7.4	−8.2	6.0
Net factor income from abroad	4.1	14.0	6.4	−1.0	4.9	−1.0	4.3
Current account balance (per cent of GDP)	−3.4	−3.5	−1.3	−2.2	−4.7	−3.1	0.1

1. Preliminary.
2. Imports of ships and aircraft, as well as imports for the aluminium and ferrosilicon plants and any imports for the public power sector.
Source: National Economic Institute.

to a sharp drop in payments for services at the Keflavik air base. Total goods and services export volumes across all sectors rose 6.1 per cent (Table 2), but earnings in foreign-currency terms rose much less, primarily due to the decline in world fish prices through September. This decline in the terms of trade was directly responsible for a drop in real national income of about 1 per cent.

Personal disposable income fell even faster than national income in 1993, due to increased personal tax rates and increased unemployment: thus private consumption plunged 4½ per cent. The weakness of current and prospective domestic demand contributed somewhat to a 29 per cent decline in business investment, but most important by far was a IKr 3.8 billion (68 per cent) cutback

Table 2. **Demand and output**

Percentage change in volume terms, 1990 prices

	1989	1990	1991	1992	1993[1]
Private consumption	−4.2	−0.4	5.1	−4.7	−4.5
Public consumption	3.0	4.2	3.2	−1.0	2.0
Gross fixed investment	−8.3	2.8	2.1	−11.2	−11.6
Business	−20.1	7.5	0.1	−12.8	−29.4
Residential	2.8	−0.6	−5.0	−3.3	−7.0
Public	5.4	−1.4	9.9	−14.1	7.9
Final domestic demand	−3.7	1.2	4.1	−5.2	−4.4
Stockbuilding[2]	−0.8	−0.3	0.8	−0.3	0.3
Total domestic demand	−4.5	0.9	5.0	−5.5	−4.2
Exports of goods and services	2.6	−0.2	−5.7	−1.7	6.1
Exports of goods	3.5	−1.4	−7.9	−1.0	5.1
Exports of services	−0.1	3.7	0.3	−3.7	8.6
Imports of goods and services	−10.0	1.0	5.6	−7.8	−8.6
Imports of goods	−10.9	0.3	4.9	−7.6	−14.1
Imports of services	−8.3	3.0	7.4	−8.2	6.0
Foreign balance[2]	4.7	−0.4	−4.3	1.8	5.0
GDP	0.2	0.5	1.0	−3.4	0.8
GNP	−0.1	0.6	0.8	−3.5	0.7
Gross national income[3]	−1.8	0.0	2.4	−4.2	−0.9
Cost of living index	21.1	14.8	6.8	3.7	4.1

1. Provisional.
2. Contribution to GDP growth, *i.e.* changes in aggregates expressed as a percentage of GDP of the previous year.
3. GNP adjusted for effects of changes in the terms of trade.
Source: National Economic Institute.

in purchases of ships by the fisheries sector. Falling incomes and rising unemployment rates also drove down residential investment – the fourth successive yearly decline. Public investment increased about 8 per cent, but this reflected primarily a transitory, one-year increase in spending on roadbuilding for purposes of job creation. Concerns about falling national income and increasing joblessness also led the government to boost maintenance expenditures and thus public consumption by 2 per cent in 1993. That, along with cyclical changes in transfers and tax receipts, led to a widening in the Treasury deficit from 1.9 to 2.4 per cent of GDP in 1993.

Last year's considerable decline in consumption demand reduced the need for imports of consumer goods. But the even sharper decline in investment was a more important drag on import demand, since investment spending is more import-intensive than is private consumption. Thus, the drop-off in import volumes was generalised but most important in ships and aircraft, and the nearly 9 per cent overall drop was so sharp that the current account actually balanced, despite the significant decline in fish export prices. But the overall balance of payments moved into deficit, as the capital account registered a net outflow, especially on private short- and long-term capital account (Table 3). Nevertheless, foreign debt in kronur terms continued to expand at a rapid pace (Table 4), reaching 56 per cent of GDP, primarily due to revaluation of foreign-currency liabilities resulting from the two devaluations of the krona. However, foreign borrowing by the public sector also played an important role (*cf.* Chapter II). In real foreign-currency terms, the debt actually fell, and the average interest rate on the debt continued to decline[6], but net interest has remained a fairly steady 11 per cent of total export revenue.

Stagnation of output and sounder monetary policy have brought consumer price inflation under control in recent years, from more than 20 per cent in the late 1980s to 4.1 per cent in 1993 (Diagram 4). The devaluations of November 1992 and June 1993 boosted the price of imported goods and created temporary surges in inflation, but underlying inflation remains much less than in previous years. Three or four months after the devaluations, consumer price inflation once more fell to very low rates; for example, it averaged only 1.2 per cent at an annual rate in the last four months of 1993. And in both December 1993 and January 1994, sizeable declines were recorded, the latter entirely

Table 3. **Balance of payments**

IKr billion

	1990	1991	1992	1993
Merchandise exports	92.5	91.6	87.8	94.7
Fish products	69.9	73.2	69.9	74.6
Aluminium and ferrosilicon	12.0	9.8	9.7	10.8
Other	10.5	8.5	8.2	9.4
Merchandise imports	87.7	94.6	87.9	82.4
Ships and aircraft	8.0	6.3	6.6	1.8
Other	79.7	88.3	81.3	80.6
Merchandise trade balance	4.8	−3.1	−0.1	12.3
Non-factor services exports	34.5	36.4	36.5	43.5
Travel	8.1	8.0	7.4	8.9
Defence force	9.2	9.4	9.8	9.1
Transportation	12.7	13.0	12.2	15.6
Other	4.4	5.9	7.1	9.9
Non-factor services imports	32.6	36.5	34.8	40.9
Travel	16.2	17.3	16.6	17.9
Transportation	10.4	11.9	10.8	12.7
Other	6.1	7.3	7.4	10.2
Non-factor services balance	1.9	−0.2	1.7	2.6
Net investment income	−14.4	−14.8	−13.6	−14.6
Unrequited transfers, net	0.0	−0.3	−0.4	−0.1
Current-account balance	−7.7	−17.7	−12.4	0.2
Direct investment, net	−0.2	1.6	0.5	0.2
Portfolio investment, net	0.0	1.3	−0.9	−2.8
Long-term borrowing, net	16.4	14.6	13.1	5.9
Public sector	5.3	11.0	10.6	6.0
Financial institutions	2.9	2.0	2.3	2.5
Private sector	8.2	1.6	0.2	−2.6
Short-term capital, net	4.0	1.5	3.0	−7.6
Public sector	−0.1	−1.4	1.5	−0.2
Financial institutions	−2.1	2.0	0.8	−3.1
Private sector	−1.9	0.9	0.7	−4.2
Capital-account balance	12.1	17.8	16.2	−6.1
Net errors and omissions	−0.0	1.3	0.7	0.1
Overall balance of payments	4.3	0.7	4.5	−5.7
of which: Central Bank reserves	4.3	0.9	4.2	−4.1

Source: Central Bank of Iceland.

Table 4. **Net external position**

IKr billion, end of period

	1990	1991	1992	1993[1]
Portfolio investment, net	–	–1.3	–0.4	2.3
Total long-term debt	176.7	191.0	228.1	264.5
Public sector	96.7	107.5	131.2	158.4
Treasury	59.5	65.8	84.5	101.9
Government enterprises	31.3	35.7	38.7	46.6
Municipalities	5.9	6.0	8.0	10.0
Financial institutions	59.4	61.6	72.3	81.3
Central Bank	0.1	0.1	0.1	0.0
Commercial banks	25.3	25.1	26.3	27.6
Investment credit funds	33.9	36.4	45.9	53.7
Private sector	20.6	22.0	24.6	24.8
Fisheries	1.0	1.0	1.8	1.6
Manufacturing	1.5	1.3	1.2	0.9
Transportation	12.9	15.6	17.5	18.2
Other	5.2	4.0	4.1	4.1
Short-term debt	21.0	22.6	24.3	18.9
Public sector	0.3	0.1	0.6	0.4
Commercial bank, relent	11.4	13.5	15.9	14.5
Private sector	9.3	9.1	7.8	4.0
Foreign assets	39.1	40.1	45.2	45.9
Public sector	0.0	1.0	0.1	0.3
Commercial banks' net liquidity	2.8	3.4	3.0	5.2
Private sector	12.8	11.6	11.1	11.8
Net foreign reserves	23.4	24.1	31.1	28.7
Net external debt position	158.6	174.8	207.6	235.1
At yearly average exchange rate	161.7	179.6	189.6	228.8
In per cent of GDP	45.6	46.8	49.5	55.8

1. Preliminary.
Source: Central Bank of Iceland.

attributable to a fall in food prices resulting from a cut in the relevant VAT rate (see Chapter II).

Labour-market conditions have deteriorated severely over the past two years: real wage rates declined, and the registered unemployment rate rose to its highest annual average since registration of unemployment began in 1969. The repercussions of this change for policy and the outlook are so important that it merits a more detailed discussion.

Diagram 4. **INFLATION PERFORMANCE**

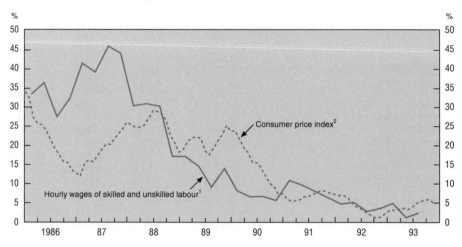

1. Percentage change from four quarters earlier.
2. Percentage change from twelve months earlier.
Source: National Economic Institute.

Labour-market deterioration

Until the past two or three years, Iceland had been extraordinarily successful in keeping unemployment to a minimum. Registered unemployment rates averaged only 0.8 per cent over the 1980s[7], despite high labour-force participation rates and growth in working-age population among the fastest in the OECD[8]. Iceland's real wage rates have been among the most flexible in the OECD, and this wage flexibility has minimised the effects of shifts in labour demand resulting from large swings in fish prices and output.

Several institutional factors have helped until recently to maintain extraordinary flexibility in Iceland's labour market. First, the Nordic countries maintain a common labour market with free access for all countries in the bloc. Thus, in past periods of weak demand for labour in Iceland, a noticeable fraction of the labour force has migrated to northern Europe. Second, the wage bill in the fisheries is tied to overall revenues from the fish catch. Thus, when revenues fall, fishing firms can maintain employment and let productivity fall without eroding the profit share[9]. Unemployment benefits are low by international standards, and thus unemployed workers may be quicker to accept jobs at lower wage rates. Finally, the labour market is highly centralised: 90 per cent of the labour force is unionised, and annual wage bargaining generally takes place at the national level. The initial stage of negotiations brings together the Icelandic Federation of Labour and the Employers' Federation, with the government often playing an active role – and subsequent bargaining sometimes occurs at the firm level[10]. In the low-inflation environment of the 1990s, the social partners have allied themselves more closely and sought a national consensus for wage moderation backed up by fiscal concessions.

During the ongoing fisheries downturn, labourers have continued the pattern of migration from rural areas to Reykjavik in search of better job opportunities, but the job openings no longer exist. Since November 1991, surveys of labour vacancies have indicated that the companies surveyed would have preferred to have almost 1 per cent fewer employees: correspondingly, the registered unemployment rate rose to 3 per cent in 1992 and reached an average of 4.3 per cent in 1993 – a level not seen for decades (Table 5). The best explanation for this deterioration is that institutional factors that supported employment during past recessions have been less effective in the current downturn. First of all, recession and increased structural unemployment in Northern Europe have prevented much emigration for jobseekers during the current downturn in Iceland – recent college graduates have been more constrained in this respect than in the past. Second, inflation rates are much lower now than in the 1980s and before: maintaining employment might now require *nominal* wage declines, which are often difficult for labour unions to accept. In the wage negotiations during the spring of 1993, the unions went only so far as to agree to a contract freezing nominal wage rates through end-1994. In the circumstances, unchanged nominal wages did not constitute as much of a concession by labour as it might appear at first sight. In fact, the negotiated zero growth in wage rates probably led to a significant rise in labour's share of national income and may have contributed to the renewed increases in unemployment later in the year, despite positive GDP growth.

The European Economic Area which has existed since January 1994 will have important implications for Iceland's labour markets. The distribution of labour income is quite compressed, relative to most OECD countries. It may be difficult for the country to maintain its egalitarian income structure, as the

Table 5. **Labour-market conditions**

	1984-86	1987	1988	1989	1990	1991	1992	1993
Labour vacancies								
Number (in thousands)	2.4	3.2	1.7	–0.3	0.0	0.2	–0.8	–0.7
Per cent of total labour force	2.6	3.5	1.9	0.4	0.0	0.2	–0.8	–0.9
Unemployment rate (per cent)								
Registered	0.9	0.5	0.6	1.7	1.8	1.5	3.0	4.3
ILO definition[1]	n.a.	n.a.	n.a.	n.a.	n.a.	2.4	3.9	5.1
Work-week of full-time manual workers[2] (hours)	50.0	50.1	47.9	48.2	47.5	47.6	47.2	47.8[4]
Man-days lost due to work stoppages (in thousands)[3]	131	99	101	80	0.2	3	0.4	n.a.
Earnings per worker (per cent change)								
Nominal	33.2	42.8	26.7	13.5	6.7	8.6	4.1	2.9[4]
Real	5.1	20.2	1.0	–6.1	–6.8	1.3	0.6	–0.4[4]

1. Average of semi-annual survey outcomes.
2. More precisely, the work-week of skilled and unskilled workers who work more than 400 hours per quarter.
3. From the *Quarterly Report* of the Wage Investigation Committee.
4. Through the second quarter.
Source: National Economic Institute; Statistical Bureau of Iceland; Nordic Council of Ministers and the Nordic Statistical Secretariat, *Yearbook of Nordic Statistics.*

regulatory changes associated with the European Economic Area come into play. The least-skilled workers are highly paid relative to most OECD countries: this will present significant labour cost problems for some Icelandic firms trying to prevent new inroads by foreign competitors. (The fish processing industry has already imported a fair amount of foreign labour, though the fisheries *per se* are exempted from the EEA rules, and EEA-related competition will certainly not be the main reason for wage declines in that sector.) Furthermore, with the EEA agreement now in force, Icelandic labour will in principle be allowed free access to EC labour markets, with Germany and the United Kingdom being two potential destinations – thus, a moderate increase in the rate of emigration of skilled workers may eventually put upward pressure on wage rates of the most skilled, and perhaps in the long run hinder the ability of the government to maintain its relatively egalitarian tax structure.

Near-term outlook

Prospects for income and output in 1994 still look relatively bleak, notwithstanding the surprising resilience of the fisheries last year. Cod quotas for the 1993/94 season were set about 30 per cent below the previous year's catch – a major shock to potential national output. Further increases in foreign fishing by the Icelandic fleet could conceivably attenuate the revenue losses, and increases in fish and aluminium prices would certainly help real incomes and tend to boost non-fisheries output. But absent such good fortune, incomes could fall sharply: the central projection, incorporating a slight improvement in the terms of trade, anticipates a decline in GDP of over 1 per cent and a similar contraction in national income (Table 6).

This year a variety of tax changes have been implemented, as discussed in Chapter II. Their net effect on real disposable income is expected to be relatively limited, however, and it may fall to about the same extent as real national income.

Table 6. **Short-term projections**

Percentage changes, volume (1990 prices)

	1994		1995
	Official forecast March 1994	OECD	OECD
Private consumption	−0.6	−0.5	1.5
Government consumption	−0.8	−0.4	1.0
Gross fixed capital formation	−1.9	−3.6	3.4
Final domestic demand	−0.8	−1.0	1.7
Change in stockbuilding[1]	−0.3	−0.2	0.0
Total domestic demand	−1.1	−1.2	1.7
Exports of goods and services	−0.8	−1.0	2.6
Imports of goods and services	−1.1	−1.0	3.4
Change in foreign balance[1]	n.a.	−0.1	−0.1
GDP	−1.1	−1.2	1.5
GDP implicit price deflator	1.2	1.4	1.4
Consumer price index	2.0	1.0	0.5
Unemployment rate (in per cent)	5.5	6.0	6.2
Current balance[2]	−0.2	0.2	0.2

1. As a percentage of GDP in the previous period.
2. As a percentage of GDP.
Source: National Economic Institute and OECD.

Consumers, however, probably anticipate some rebound in income in future years, so that a small further decline in saving rates seems likely this year – personal consumption is projected to fall 0.5 per cent. Demand for housing will be affected by the continuing weakness in disposable income, but lower mortgage interest rates may offset the income drop: spending on residential investment is not expected to fall much further this year. Businesses considering investing in 1994 will have to take into account the probable weakness of sales volumes; however, corporate tax rates have been reduced further for 1994, and this may buttress business investment outlays. Public investment will decline fairly sharply as the government winds down a temporary 1993 roadbuilding programme. Real public consumption is also budgeted to fall in 1994, as the government tries to hold down the Treasury deficit and control the burgeoning public debt. Thus, private consumption, total investment and public consumption are all expected to turn down in 1994, resulting in a projected decline in total domestic demand of about 1.2 per cent.

The sharp drop in cod quotas for 1993/94 may lead to a fall in merchandise export volumes in 1994, even with the best efforts of fishing firms to broaden the scope of their fishing efforts. Some increase is probable in services exports, especially tourism, but overall export volumes are projected to decline by about 1 per cent. However, import volumes should also fall with declining real national income: on balance, no change in the current account balance – at about 0.2 per cent of GDP – is expected. With falling GDP and no further improvement in the current account, net foreign debt may rise – according to the Central Bank to 60 per cent of GDP by year-end.

The weakness in overall activity this year is likely to cause further deterioration in the labour market: the unemployment rate is expected to increase to 6 per cent for the year as a whole. With continuing softness in labour demand, any drift away from the 1993 agreement on wage rates is likely to be downward. Stable unit labour costs will therefore be one factor holding down inflation. Also, inflation was very low going into 1994, and consequently the "carry-over" is minimal. The recession is likely to cut into companies' mark-ups, and, finally, January's sharp drop in the VAT rate on food more than offset the impact on inflation of the implementation of VAT on hotels and travel services. Overall, the rise in consumer prices may be held to no more than 1 per cent in both 1994 and 1995.

II.   Economic policies

Continuing fiscal slippage

Recent outcomes

When the cod catch peaked in 1987, Treasury debt was about 24 per cent of GDP and the deficit came to 1.3 per cent of GDP. However, the downturn in the fisheries over the past six years has put increasing pressure on government revenues, while government expenditures have expanded significantly in real terms, especially in 1991. Thus, between 1988 and 1990, the Treasury deficit increased to 2 per cent of GDP on average, and the gross Treasury debt rose to about 32 per cent of GDP in 1990. This level of debt was still far from serious; however, the fiscal situation deteriorated sharply the following year, when the authorities expanded agricultural subsidies and postponed planned tax increases and spending cuts until after the April 1991 elections. As a result, the Treasury deficit soared, reaching 3.3 per cent of GDP in 1991 (Table 7).

The current government came into power determined to reverse the fiscal excesses of 1991, despite signs of weakening economic conditions. Some fiscal consolidation was achieved in 1992, *via* cut-backs in government consumption, investment, subsidies and social-security transfers – along with increases in user fees and reductions in personal tax credits. The Treasury deficit fell to 1.9 per cent of GDP, but this was a disappointment relative to the target of 1 per cent. The underlying culprit for the shortfall was the continuing decline in real earnings of the fisheries, which weakened labour income and the tax base more than had been expected, putting tremendous pressure on Treasury balances. Even with the narrower deficit of 1992, the gross public debt jumped by 7$\frac{1}{2}$ percentage points relative to GDP[11], reaching 45 per cent. The speed of this deterioration, more than the absolute size of the debt (which is moderate), has limited the fiscal options available to counteract further the ongoing recession.

Table 7. **Treasury finances**

IKr million, cash basis

	1991	1992 Budget	1992 Outcome	1992 Difference	1992 % Difference	1993 Budget	1993 Outcome	1993 Difference	1993 % Difference	1993/1992 %	1994 Budget	1994 Budget/1993 Budget %	1994 Budget/1993 Outcome %
Total revenue	99 953	105 463	103 447	-2 016	-1.9	104 771	103 220	-1 551	-1.5	-0.2	104 146	-0.6	0.9
Direct taxes	19 263	21 088	20 348	-740	-3.5	20 193	20 311	118	0.6	-0.2	21 345	5.7	5.1
Indirect taxes	74 240	76 215	75 422	-793	-1.0	76 698	75 851	-847	-1.1	0.6	75 376	-1.7	-0.6
Import duties and excises	9 460	8 608	8 195	-413	-4.8	8 656	7 695	-961	-11.1	-6.1	7 934	-8.3	3.1
VAT	38 954	40 450	39 944	-506	-1.3	40 950	40 497	-453	-1.1	1.4	38 815	-5.2	-4.2
Other	25 826	27 157	27 283	126	0.5	27 092	27 659	567	2.1	1.4	28 627	5.7	3.5
Other revenue	6 450	8 160	7 677	-483	-6.0	7 880	7 058	-822	-10.4	-8.1	7 425	-5.8	5.2
Total expenditure	112 487	109 575	110 607	1 032	0.9	111 015	112 863	1 848	1.7	2.0	113 782	2.5	0.8
Consumption	44 705	43 877	44 923	1 046	2.4	46 478	47 855	1 377	3.0	6.5	46 473	-0.0	-2.9
Transfer payments	45 109	43 925	46 243	2 318	5.3	41 252	42 952	1 700	4.1	-7.1	44 031	6.7	2.5
Social security	28 265	26 826	28 716	1 890	7.0	27 754	29 013	1 259	4.5	1.0	29 479	6.2	1.6
Agricultural subsidies	9 049	8 264	9 432	1 168	14.1	6 191	6 518	327	5.3	-30.9	5 752	-7.1	-11.8
Other	7 795	8 835	8 095	-740	-8.4	7 307	7 421	114	1.6	-8.3	8 800	20.4	18.6
Interest payments	9 875	9 900	8 346	-1 554	-15.7	10 500	9 732	-768	-7.3	16.6	11 450	9.0	17.7
Capital expenditure	12 798	11 873	11 095	-778	-6.6	12 786	12 323	-463	-3.6	11.1	11 828	-7.5	-4.0
Revenue balance[1]	12 534	4 112	7 160	3 048	74.1	6 244	9 643	3 399	54.4	34.7	9 636	54.3	-0.1
Percentage of GDP	3.3	1.1	1.9			1.7	2.4				2.4		
Treasury net borrowing requirement[2]	14 648	4 900	7 175	2 275	46.4	8 939	10 698	1 759	19.7	49.1	11 776	31.7	10.1
Percentage of GDP	3.8	1.3	1.9			2.2	2.7				3.0		
Public-sector borrowing requirement[3]	40 200	19 200	23 800	4 600	24.0	26 000	23 200	-2 800	-10.8	-2.5	22 700	-12.7	-2.2
Percentage of GDP	10.5	5.0	6.2			6.5	5.8				5.7		

1. Equals total expenditure less total revenue.
2. Equals the revenue balance plus net Treasury lending, equity purchases and short-term credit.
3. Equals the Treasury net borrowing requirement plus the net borrowing of public-sector financial and non-financial institutions, including that of municipalities, which is very small.

Source: Ministry of Finance.

The primary goal of the 1993 budget was to slow the growth of government indebtedness, by reducing the Treasury deficit to 1.6 per cent of GDP. This target reduction of only 0.3 percentage point might seem small, but it was in fact quite ambitious, in light of the lower catch quotas for cod and probable weakness of national income. The budget passed at year-end 1992 did indeed contain a variety of tightening measures. On the spending side, subsidies were trimmed and social-security transfers were to be cut, counterbalancing planned increases in public-works spending to reduce job losses. Revenues were increased by a broadening of the VAT to cover several previously exempt items, a reduction in mortgage interest rebates, and the abolition of corporate investment tax credits (the ''investment funds''). Several other tax and subsidy reforms were made with the aim of improving competitiveness and harmonising Iceland's fiscal code with EEA and GATT standards. This was to be achieved primarily by the abolition of the ''turnover tax'' on business operating costs, and a phased reduction in corporate income tax rates, which had previously been well above the European average[12]. However, abolition of the local turnover tax cost municipalities some IKr 4 billion in revenues. The government made up these losses by implementing several other tax increases, and passing the revenues on to the municipalities[13].

On balance, these tightening measures in the budget were expected to outweigh the revenue losses from tax reforms – but the course of events in 1993 contained some unpleasant fiscal surprises. Within a few weeks of its passage, the first adjustment to the budget was made. On 10 January, the government scrapped its plan to reduce rebates on the VAT for residential investment projects. This change in the budget served to erode 1993 revenues by IKr 400 million, or 0.1 per cent of GDP. However, more serious fiscal problems arose in May. By that point, the unemployment rate had risen to nearly 5 per cent, noticeably higher than the 3.4 per cent rate assumed in the budget. Given the worsening employment situation, the government chose to make fiscal concessions as it had often done in the past in order to help finalise the national wage negotiations between employers and the federation of labour unions. The most important measure having effect in 1993 was the temporary abolition of the social-security tax on export industries, costing the Treasury IKr 330 million. Also, indirectly related to these concessions was the lowering of excise duties on construction materials and automobiles, at a total cost of IKr 300 million. Expenditure concessions were significantly larger: a IKr 1 billion increase in appropriations for public investment to boost employment[14], greater transfer payments to low-income households and temporarily higher subsidies on agricultural products, as a precursor to the general reduction in VAT on food products from 24.5 to 14 per cent as from 1 January 1994. Total concessions due to the May wage agreement amounted to about IKr 2.2 billion in 1993, or 0.6 per cent of GDP.

One of the 1993 budget assumptions was privatisation of the government-owned Agricultural Bank together with those of a few other public enterprises. However, concerns arose about the risk of making changes in the country's banking system during the severe economic contraction, which has been reflected in the unfavourable state of the Icelandic stock market. Thus, this sell-off was postponed, resulting in a total revenue shortfall of nearly IKr 1.5 billion in 1993.

Deteriorating economic conditions created other significant gaps in the budget over the course of the year. The most severe slippage resulted from the unexpected severity of employment losses. The government had anticipated that the unemployment rate would rise to 3.4 per cent with economic weakness, but the annual average rate was actually 4.3 per cent[15]. As a result, transfer payments for unemployment insurance were IKr 700 million higher than planned. Furthermore, the decline in national income eroded income tax receipts more than expected[16]. In all, weakness of employment and income led to an underestimate of the budget deficit by about IKr 2 billion, or 0.5 per cent of GDP. This employment weakness, combined with the above-mentioned fiscal concessions and privatisation postponement, contributed to a total overrun in the Treasury deficit amounting to IKr 3.4 billion[17]. The actual deficit was much higher than the budgeted figure, rising to 2.4 per cent of GDP rather than falling to 1.6 per cent. Gross Treasury debt rose to over 45 per cent of GDP in 1993, an increase of nearly 6 percentage points. About one-third of that rise is attributable to the June devaluation of the krona. Excluding Treasury relending, the net debt of the Treasury is much lower, only about 27 per cent of GDP. This is well below the OECD average.

Treasury relending, at 0.3 per cent of GDP, was, however, a bit less than anticipated, and the housing funds' net borrowing was also less than had been expected. Thus, the public sector borrowing requirement (PSBR), at 5.5 per cent of GDP, was lower than the forecast level of 6.7 per cent and, in fact, the lowest since 1987 (Table 8). Nonetheless, this relatively high PSBR, along with the June

Table 8. **Public-sector borrowing requirement**[1]

	1987	1988	1989	1990	1991	1992	1993	1994
	IKr billion, net							
Total	11.6	17.0	22.9	27.0	40.2	23.8	21.8	22.7
Treasury	5.5	8.2	7.5	7.9	14.7	7.2	10.7	11.8
Revenue balance	2.7	7.1	6.0	4.4	12.5	7.2	9.6	9.6
Net lending, etc.	2.8	1.1	1.5	3.5	2.1	0.0	1.1	2.1
Housing system	3.8	6.1	8.0	14.2	22.2	15.9	13.0	12.5
Other	2.3	2.7	7.4	4.9	3.3	0.7	−1.9	−1.6
	Percentage of GDP							
Total	5.6	6.7	7.5	7.6	10.5	6.2	5.5	5.7
Treasury	2.7	3.3	2.5	2.3	3.8	1.9	2.7	3.0
Revenue balance	1.3	2.8	2.0	1.3	3.3	1.9	2.4	2.4
Net lending, etc.	1.4	0.5	0.5	1.0	0.6	0.0	0.3	0.6
Housing system	1.8	2.4	2.6	4.0	5.8	4.1	3.3	3.1
Other	1.1	1.1	2.4	1.4	0.9	0.2	−0.5	−0.4

1. Including the financing of the housing system.
Source: Ministry of Finance.

devaluation, resulted in a sharp increase in the gross public debt ratio, to 51 per cent of GDP. This is certainly not yet anywhere near dangerous levels. Nonetheless, over the past two years the debt ratio has increased by almost 14 percentage points – a rate that cannot be sustained indefinitely.

The 1994 budget

In planning the 1994 budget, the government had the unenviable task of trying to restrain the recent rapid increases in public debt in a period of falling real national income – and simultaneously limiting employment losses. The expected downturn in employment and income limited the room for manœuvre in reducing the deficit further in 1994. The proposed Treasury revenue balance amounts to 2.4 per cent of GDP, compared to the 3.2 per cent expected for 1993 when the budget was debated but virtually identical to the actual 1993 outcome. The budget anticipates substantial growth of unemployment insurance outlays in 1994, but proposes even larger cuts in other spending categories. Revenue is projected to rise slightly in nominal terms, despite the ongoing recession, mainly due to spillovers from 1993 tax changes of IKr 1.5 billion. In real terms, however, Treasury revenues are expected to fall slightly.

The largest change on the revenue side in the 1994 budget was a lowering of VAT on food products from 24.5 per cent to 14 per cent effective as of 1 January. This was one of the main measures of the government's concessions made to facilitate general wage agreements last spring. To compensate for the reduction of the VAT, other tax measures were legislated at year-end 1993. The personal income tax rate was raised by 0.35 percentage point, the weight-based annual levy on automobiles was increased by 30 per cent and the social-security tax on employers was raised by 0.35 percentage point. On the whole, these measures are estimated to reduce the Treasury revenues by approximately IKr 1.2 billion in 1994. Another factor affecting the Treasury revenue in 1994 is the permanent arrangement of the tax reshuffling between the central government and the municipalities. This entails a cut of 1.5 percentage points in personal income tax rates and the abolition of national business property taxes. Finally, there are several changes carried over from the 1993 budget. Thus, the corporate income tax rate was reduced from 39 to 33 per cent in 1994, interest rebates for residential housing were lowered and a 14 per cent VAT was introduced on hotel services[18].

The main emphasis of the 1994 budget is, however, a continuing curtailment of total expenditures. These include further reductions in agricultural subsidies, a considerable cut in operating costs[19] and most significantly a sharp reduction in public investment expenditure (primarily a winding down of most of the 1993 expansion in road construction). As a result of recurrent Treasury deficits in the past, the interest payments on the Treasury debt will rise substantially in 1994, though the late-1993 reduction in long-term interest rates reduces the expected size of the increase by about IKr 300 million. This fact and increased unemployment benefits explain a slight nominal increase of Treasury expenditures in 1994. In real terms, however, expenditures are estimated to decrease marginally.

If all goes as planned, the PSBR will rise in 1994 by 0.2 per cent of GDP, similar to the marginal increase in the Treasury deficit. The increase puts the projected PSBR for 1994 at 5.7 per cent of GDP, another high level compared to the Treasury deficit. The difference primarily reflects government borrowing to finance housing loans. Fundamentally, however, the government is acting as an

Diagram 5. **GROSS PUBLIC DEBT RATIO**[1]

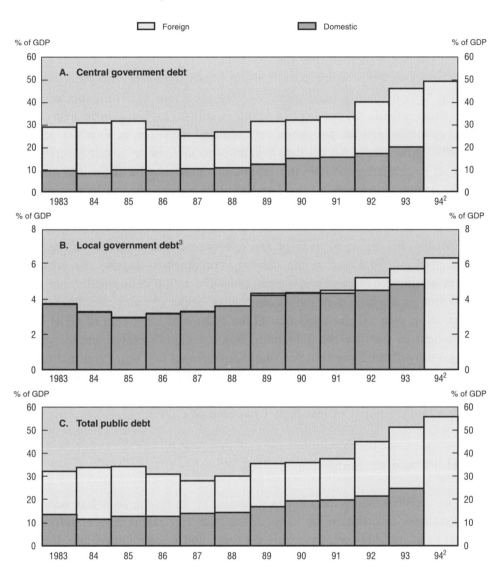

1. Per cent of GDP. Relending has varied between 18 and 28 per cent of GDP. Thus net debt of the central government will have increased from 6 per cent in 1983 to 30 per cent in 1994; at the same time net debt of all levels of government will have risen from 5 to 33 per cent of GDP.
2. Foreign/domestic split unavailable.
3. Estimate.
Source: Ministry of Finance.

31

intermediary in the housing market, and the PSBR figures (which include mortgage bonds and the activities of the Housing Funds) may therefore be less relevant than the Treasury deficit as a measure of underlying pressure of government borrowing on national saving.

Whether or not one includes housing bonds, however, the public debt is expected to rise sharply once more in 1994 (Diagram 5). The expected gross public debt, roughly 56 per cent of GDP, is still no higher than in many other OECD countries, and the net public debt remains far lower, at about 33 per cent of GDP[20]. However, if the net debt continues to increase by about 5 percentage points per year relative to GDP, the debt burden may soon be difficult to manage. In 1994, interest payments on the Treasury debt are expected to increase 16 per cent in real terms, reaching more than 10 per cent of total Treasury expenditure and 2.9 per cent of GDP. It may not be easy for the government to consolidate its fiscal position in coming years if the severe economic circumstances of the recent past persist and weakness in the fisheries continues to depress the economy. Were economic growth and real interest rates to develop in line with those in the OECD area as a whole over the medium term (about 2½ to 3 and 3½ per cent, respectively), then a Treasury deficit in the order of 2½ per cent of GDP would be sufficient to stabilise the debt ratio. But if Iceland's real economic growth averages only about 2 per cent per year over the next few years and real interest rates continue to exceed those in the rest of the OECD by a wide margin due to the narrowness of financial markets, then Treasury debt stabilisation would require a budget deficit of less than 1 per cent of GDP[21].

Monetary and exchange-rate policy

The problem facing the monetary authorities in recent years has been two-fold: first, how to maintain the value of the exchange rate at a level sufficiently high so as to put downward pressure on wage and price inflation and complete the disinflation process under way since 1988, but not so high as to cause competitiveness problems and resulting balance-of-payments and foreign indebtedness difficulties; second, how to introduce a greater role for markets in determining interest rates with a view to bringing down their unusually high level in inflation-adjusted terms (this would help the economy to expand and relieve the interest burden on the national Treasury). The two have been recognised as interconnected: the more stable the actual and expected values of the exchange rate, the greater the credibility of monetary policy and the lower interest rates are likely to be.

Another adjustment of the krona peg

Over the first half of 1993 monetary and exchange-rate policy continued to be guided, as it had been in 1990-92, largely by the intermediate objective of exchange-rate stability. The devaluation of November 1992 – formally 6 per cent but only about 4½ per cent in effective terms – was a direct response to the turmoil on European foreign exchange markets that autumn. It was seen as a one-off adjustment needed to avoid the risk of a downward spiral of activity, to rein in excessive national expenditure relative to income and to bolster the profitability of the fisheries sector. There followed a brief period of interest-rate and price increases resulting from the readjustment of the peg, but thereafter markets settled down in anticipation of a lengthy period of stability, even if the start of trading on the new interbank foreign-exchange market on 28 May allowed fluctuations within a band of 2¼ per cent on each side of the central parity[22].

However, the calm was broken in June when the Marine Research Institute recommended that the cod catch be cut back by 27 per cent in 1993-94, followed shortly by the government's acquiescence to a cut of 20 per cent in the total allowable catch. Furthermore, export prices for fish had resumed their slide already in the late summer of 1992 and by June, 1993 were nearly 20 per cent in SDR terms below their levels of the beginning of 1992. The real exchange rate of the krona consistent with these fundamentals was seen by the authorities as inconsistent with the policy of continued fixity in the nominal exchange rate, and therefore on 28 June they announced a further devaluation of 7.5 per cent of the central rate[23] (Diagram 6, panel A). Again, a brief uptick in inflation and interest rates ensued, but the krona managed a slight recovery, finishing the year about ½ per cent higher than its mid-year level, albeit nearly 12 per cent below the level which prevailed prior to the 1992 devaluation[24].

The two devaluations of 1992-93 have left the real value of the krona at very low levels by historical standards – in terms of relative unit labour costs its current value is at its lowest level in at least three decades, and barely half what it was prior to the collapse of herring stocks in the late 1960s and one-third below its previous peak in 1988. On a relative consumer-price basis it is at its lowest

Diagram 6. **NOMINAL AND EFFECTIVE EXCHANGE RATE OF THE KRONA**

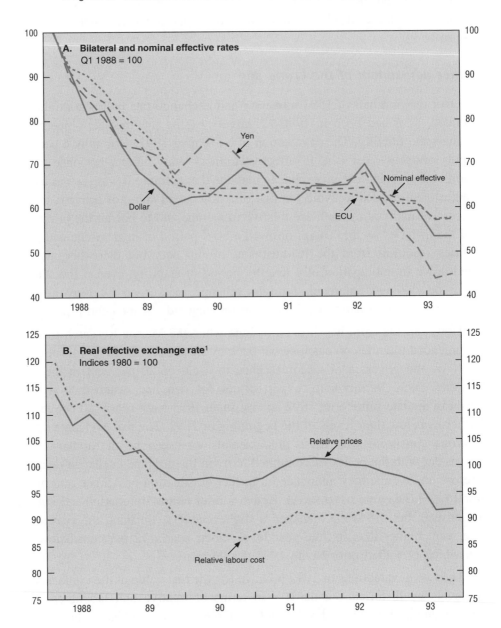

1. Estimates for 1993 are from the Central Bank of Iceland.
Source: Central Bank of Iceland.

Table 9. **The index of competitive position**

	Fishing sector	Manufacturing export sector	Domestic manufacturing sector	Average
1979	100.0	100.0	100.0	100.0
1980	95.0	107.8	97.6	96.6
1981	94.4	103.6	96.9	95.7
1982	91.3	106.3	97.5	93.8
1983	99.6	116.6	108.5	102.9
1984	95.9	112.3	107.2	99.7
1985	100.2	106.8	106.6	102.2
1986	106.1	96.8	106.1	105.4
1987	99.3	89.9	98.0	98.3
1988	90.3	94.3	95.4	91.8
1989	92.8	100.3	101.3	95.3
1990	101.0[1]	88.0	104.6	100.7[1]
1991	104.5[1]	82.7	101.8	102.2[1]
1992	103.0[1]	80.9	101.7	100.9[1]
1993[2]	99.2	84.8	106.6	99.7
1994[3]	102.6	89.1	111.1	103.4

1. Including the effects of the Fisheries Price Equalisation Fund which had the following impact on the index for the fishing sector: –0.7 per cent, –2.3 per cent and +2.8 per cent in 1990, 1991 and 1992, respectively.
2. Provisional.
3. Based on the following assumptions for 1994: wage change 0.0 per cent, domestic input price increase 1.4 per cent, fuel price decrease 5.5 per cent, fisheries export price increase 1.0 per cent, manufactured export price increase 2.5 per cent, exchange rate depreciation 5.2 per cent.
Source: Central Bank of Iceland.

level since 1971, about 12 per cent below its recent early-1992 peak and more than 20 per cent below peak 1988 levels (Diagram 6, panel B). The implications for competitiveness are obvious: the potential for endogenous economic diversification has been given a boost. This is also reflected in the Central Bank's index of competitive position (Table 9). With continuing weakness in export prices, not only in fish but also in the manufacturing sector and renewed declines in the real value of the fish catch (see Chapter I), it is only in small-scale, largely import-competing manufacturing that profitability has risen to attractive, indeed record, levels. Competitiveness has also been enhanced by the sharp cuts in the corporate income tax rate and the abolition of the turnover tax.

Accelerating declines in interest rates

1993 was another year of declining interest rates, but progress was rather modest until November (Diagram 7). The year's first auction of three-month

Diagram 7. **INTEREST RATE DEVELOPMENTS**

Per cent, end of month

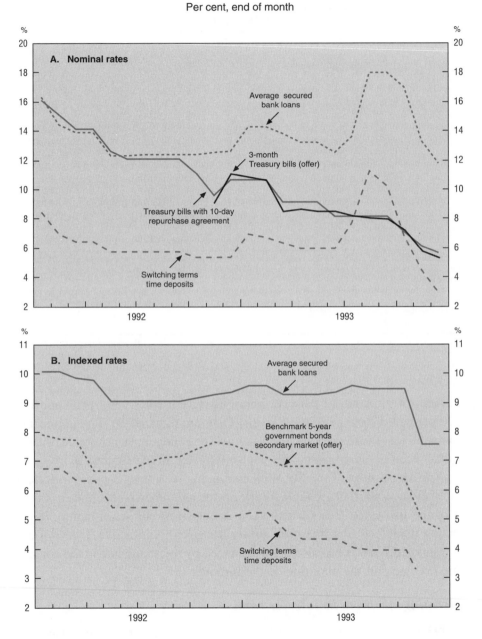

Source: Central Bank of Iceland.

Treasury bills brought a weighted yield of nearly 12.0 per cent, up from 9.3 per cent when such auctions began in November 1992; the rise resulted from higher inflation expectations pursuant to the November devaluation. Government bond yields had peaked just prior to the devaluation at nearly 8 per cent (in real terms)[25]. Rates eased fairly steadily through the winter, until the Central Bank decided on 24 March to lower its lending rates to the deposit money banks (DMBs) by 1 to 3 percentage points, to boost its bids for government paper on the secondary market in order to bring about a decline of 1.5 percentage points (to 9 per cent) in the repurchase (repo) rate and to increase the interest paid on required reserves from 2 per cent to $3^{1}/_{2}$ per cent in inflation adjusted terms. Two further half-point declines in the repo rate occurred in June. Despite a temporary uptick of around 0.8 percentage point after the June devaluation, rates on short-term government debt continued to recede moderately through the end of October, but little in the way of further declines were achieved at the long end of the term structure.

Then, on 21 October, the Central Bank agreed to cut the repo rate by a further point, and on 29 October the government announced it would no longer accept any offers for government bonds implying yields in excess of 5 per cent in inflation-adjusted terms, threatening to finance its borrowing requirement on international markets if domestic supply proved inadequate. The threat was credible because the Treasury's net borrowing requirement in 1994 was expected to fall by IKr 2.1 and the overall PSBR by IKr 4.3 billion. Lower real and nominal interest rates were also justified by the improvement in the external accounts and the return to a largely stable price level. For its part the Central Bank announced it would support the move in the secondary market, and on 8 November followed this up with a cut in the DMBs' liquidity requirement (from 12 to 10 per cent, the first change since June 1990) and in their reserve requirement (last modified in December 1992) on liquid deposits (from 5 to 4 per cent) and on deposits with notice provisions of greater than three months (from 5 to 2.5 per cent)[26]. The effect of these moves was dramatic (Table 10): real yields on government bonds on the secondary market dropped immediately by 1 percentage point and indeed at the following auction fell a further 1.2 points to 5 per cent, down by a third from January and a ten-year low. Interest rates on shorter-term non-indexed debt declined nearly in tandem: three-month bills at the year's final auction in Decem-

Table 10. **Interest-rate declines in 1993**

Per cent

	End of 1992	25.10.93	Changes from end of 1992 to 25.10.93	End of 1993	Changes from 25.10.93 to end of 1993	Changes during 1993
Indexed rates						
Secondary market:						
Government bonds, offer	7.5	7.0	–0.6	4.7	–2.3	–2.8
Housing bonds, offer	7.5	7.1	–0.4	5.4	–1.7	–2.1
Primary market:						
Goverment bonds, auctions	7.7	7.2	–0.5	5.0	–2.2	–2.7
Bank loans	9.3	9.4	0.1	7.5	–1.9	–1.8
Non-indexed rates						
Central bank:						
Repurchase rate, yield	10.5	7.0	–3.5	5.5	–1.5	–5.0
Inter-bank rate	11.3	7.8	–3.5	5.7	–2.1	–5.6
Secondary market:						
3-month Treasury bills, offer	11.1	7.2	–3.9	5.3	–1.9	–5.8
Primary market:						
3-month Treasury bills, auctions	11.9	8.1	–3.8	5.4	–2.7	–6.4
Bank loans:						
Bills of exchange, discount rates	12.0	16.7	4.7	11.8	–4.9	–0.2
General loans, bonds	12.5	16.9	4.4	11.7	–5.2	–0.8

Source: Central Bank of Iceland.

ber brought (nominal) yields of less than 5½ per cent, less than half January's outcomes.

Rates intermediated through the banking system evolved somewhat differently. Although there was a slight downtrend in indexed lending rates in the first part of the year, these remained very onerous at over 9 per cent prior to the October policy moves, with unusually wide margins of about 2½ percentage points over real returns on government bonds. Unindexed loan rates slid from 14.6 per cent in January to 12.4 per cent just before the June devaluation. But then somewhat surprisingly, the DMBs boosted these rates in the summer to nearly 18 per cent in the aftermath of the brief price surge following the devaluation. The explanation is that for the past decade the banks have held a higher proportion of their liabilities than their assets in indexed form – most recently about 68 *versus* 46 per cent, respectively – and they, therefore, try to offset the profit squeeze they face from an even temporary unexpected acceleration in inflation through such a rise in rates.

The authorities responded to this perverse situation first in July by changing the rules on indexation of deposits and loans[27], and then in September by negotiating a series of interest rate swap contracts with the DMBs with a view to shifting the inflation-induced profit risk to the Central Bank and encouraging the banks to reduce their balance-sheet mismatch over the 28-month period covered (until end-1995). At the end of each four-month period, the DMBs will pay the Central Bank a fixed nominal interest rate and receive in return a real rate plus an inflation compensation component, all this on a reference amount. The initial reference amount is the estimated DMBs' balance-sheet mismatch (about IKr 24.5 billion), but it is to be reduced by one-seventh for each subsequent four-month period. The initial inflation compensation was 2 per cent at an annual rate for the four-months ending in January 1994, as measured by the credit terms index. In the event, the index rose at only a 1.2 per cent rate, producing a handsome profit for the Central Bank. In any event, the agreements succeeded in convincing the DMBs to drop their non-indexed loan rates by 1 percentage point in early October. Then, following the policy change, intermediated rates also fell sharply: nearly 2 percentage points for real rates and over 5 points for non-indexed rates. Nevertheless, intermediation margins, already substantial at end-1992, would seem to have widened during 1993.

Signs of life in money and credit

Paralleling the accelerating declines in interest rates and the modest uptick in activity and – through October – in inflation, most monetary and credit aggregates have begun to display greater strength (Table 11). Year-on-year changes in narrow money (M1) reached a trough of about –6 per cent in the spring before recovering to finish the year with a gain of 5.6 per cent. The broader aggregates showed a similar pattern of acceleration beginning in the spring. Only base money remains firmly in a declining trend, due primarily to the recent reductions in required reserves. For its part the banking system also picked up the pace of its lending as the year wore on. With a resumption in their deposit growth, the DMBs have been able to slow the growth of their bond issuance and cut back on foreign borrowing. The investment credit funds continue to be aggressive lenders and have now surpassed the DMBs in overall lending levels.

Table 11. **Growth in monetary and credit aggregates**[1]

Per cent

	1990	1991	1992	1993
Money				
Base money	−18.1	9.6	−9.5	−12.0
M1	24.9	19.9	1.3	5.6
M3	14.9	14.4	3.8	6.2
M4[2]	15.9	13.5	4.2	6.7
Banking system lending[3]	9.6	12.4	3.2	9.3
of which: Deposit money banks	11.0	11.5	5.7	7.4
Credit				
Total	12.5	15.4	11.1	11.5
of which claims on:				
Central government	12.5	23.8	17.4	28.3[4]
Municipalities	5.7	12.9	12.3	11.3[4]
Business	5.9	8.0	7.9	6.0[4]
Households	25.8	23.7	12.9	11.8[4]
of which originating from:				
Domestic saving	18.8	18.6	8.8	10.0[4]
Voluntary	18.8	20.1	4.6	7.8[4]
Contractual	19.0	17.3	12.7	11.9[4]
Foreign credit, net	1.4	8.6	16.5	14.8[4]

1. Through-the-year growth.
2. M3 plus deposit money banks' issuance of bonds.
3. Including foreign funds relent and Central Bank lending to the Treasury.
4. Preliminary.
Source: Central Bank of Iceland.

They have financed this expansion through indexed bonds and foreign borrowing and seem intent on issuing foreign-currency bonds as well. Overall credit growth has also picked up. Preliminary data indicate that for the first time in many years households have been a restraining influence in that their borrowing has lagged that of other sectors. This is consistent with the weakness in personal disposable income and consumption over the period. Business credit demand has strengthened, but most of the extra borrowing in 1993 was undertaken by the central government and most has been provided from foreign sources[28]. Domestic saving growth remains moderate, with continuing weakness in voluntary saving due to the poor financial condition of households.

Other structural changes in financial markets

A number of other structural changes in financial markets have been effected over the past year or so. The beginning of 1993 saw a further liberalisation of capital movements. First, all flows related to international trade in goods and services were freed from regulation unless explicitly provided for by law. Second, all long-term loan transactions were fully liberalised. Short-term flows, according to the legislation, were fully restricted in 1993 with the exception of transactions on behalf of DMBs related to the interbank foreign exchange market set up in 1993. A partial relaxation of controls took place at the beginning of 1994. After 1994, the Central Bank can only regulate short-term flows for up to six months if it determines that they are causing instability in domestic monetary affairs. Third, outward flows for direct investment and purchases of residences were completely freed up, but some restrictions remain on inward direct investments[29]. Fourth, during 1993 only, there were temporary ceilings on outward long-term portfolio investments and on total bank deposits in foreign banks, except for firms with operations abroad. Fifth, foreigners were allowed to open foreign-currency accounts in Iceland, but until 1995 are permitted to hold kronur accounts only if they have operations in the country. A new basic law on foreign direct investment is due by 1 January 1996.

In March 1993 new legislation was passed regulating securities transactions, the Stock Exchange and mutual funds. Effective in July, it has brought Iceland's legal provisions in these areas into line with common international practice. In July the Central Bank widened the possibilities for repurchase agreements with the DMBs when it began to offer to buy government bonds and housing bonds as well as Treasury bills. On-tap sales of Treasury bills ceased at the end of June, and those of other short-term Treasury debt ended in August. New non-indexed 6- and 12-month bills and 24-month notes were added to the Treasury's debt-management arsenal in November, thereby helping to reduce the prevalence of indexation in Iceland's economy. As of the 1994 Credit Budget, the Treasury's borrowing authorisation is no longer segregated between domestic and foreign components, and the authorities are now able to borrow wherever cost considerations dictate. The domestic money market, which began late in 1992, has expanded rapidly since then, with turnover reaching nearly IKr 60 billion in 1993. Also, in October one of the DMBs issued foreign-currency bonds on the domestic market, something never before undertaken. Overall, turnover on and capitalisation of the domestic bond and equity markets have also surged in recent years. Finally, late in the year legislation was passed dealing with non-bank credit institutions, mainly the investment credit funds and leasing funds. Other than a ban on deposit-taking, they are now subject to the same provisions as the DMBs (and can, therefore, make long-term loans) and likewise are henceforth to be supervised by the Central Bank. It is hoped that the desegmentation of these funds might lower interest rates and intermediation margins by boosting competition.

Other plans remain in abeyance. The most important are further revisions to the Central Bank Act designed to augment the range of instruments available to implement monetary policy, to enhance its independence by removing the need for ministerial approval for their use and to clarify its objectives: rather than a multiplicity of goals, that of price stability would be given clear primacy. It would also be charged with promoting efficiency and security on financial markets, maintaining adequate foreign-currency reserves and ensuring effective payment mechanisms. The 1992 agreement preventing the Bank from providing credit to the Treasury or other public authorities would also be put into legislative form. This is intended to provide added fiscal discipline and monetary control. Other proposals aim at transforming two sectoral investment credit funds into an investment bank and at reducing the use of Treasury guarantees to mitigate the distortionary effects they have on interest-rate determination[30].

Structural policy reforms in other domains

While the authorities' attention has been focused on preparing for the entry into force of the European Economic Area (EEA) agreement at the beginning of 1994 and meeting the requirements the EEA imposed on its financial markets, they have been active in a number of other structural domains. Those related to agriculture, resource management and the environment are discussed in detail in Chapter III. Otherwise, an important new competition law was passed in February 1993, replacing the previous legislation passed in 1978. It aims to prevent unreasonable limitations to economic operation, unfair trade practices and restriction of competition and to facilitate market entry. A Competition Council, a Competition Authority and a Competition Appeals Committee have been established, replacing the Price Control Board; the Authority is the principal administrative body, while the Council has decision-making powers. Carrying on prohibited activities may incur penalties of up to IKr 500 000 (about $7 000) per day and fines can range up to IKr 40 million, or up to 10 per cent of turnover in the previous calendar year should the illegal gains exceed the IKr 40 million threshold. Henceforth, publicly owned firms in competitive sectors must keep separate accounts for their different activities to prevent hidden cross-subsidisation.

The authorities have also decided to modify the nation's science and technology policy with a view to achieving greater economic diversification. More public resources are to be channelled into this area, and the Science and Research Councils are to be merged. In a related matter, the Export Council has been directed to increase its co-operation with other agencies, including the Tourist Board, and to promote inward direct investment opportunities for foreign firms. Finally, plans are being formulated for the creation of a customs free zone.

Labour-market policy

With unemployment rates averaging less than 1 per cent prior to 1992, there was no call for the government to implement active labour-market policies[31]. When overall unemployment rates rose to nearly 5 per cent at the end of 1992, however, additional measures were deemed necessary. In November 1992, the government introduced public works measures targeted at boosting employment. Also, a new workplace training programme was introduced, with the government helping to organise courses to improve specialised skills. Finally, local governments also initiated special employment-enhancing programmes.

Other labour-market programmes have been more restrictive in Iceland than in other OECD countries: union membership was required to receive unemployment insurance benefits, and income replacement is relatively modest. The maximum duration of benefits for an initial spell is 52 weeks, and no benefits are paid in the following 16 weeks, before eligibility is renewed and the cycle repeated. However, effective 1 September 1993, the government broadened eligibility for unemployment insurance. Union membership is no longer necessary, and the regulations no longer discriminate as much against the self-employed, although to receive benefits they must still fully shut down their business. Furthermore, the unemployed now have the option of taking temporary job training courses, and thereby avoiding loss of benefits. Finally, the directors of the unemployment insurance fund can make grants to pay for the transfer of workers from one kind of work to another and for changes in residence to help workers obtain a new job. So far, no such grants have been made, pending establishment of more detailed procedures for implementation.

Though explicit intervention has been minimal until recently, the government has intervened implicitly in regional labour markets in several ways. It has slowed the exit of labour from rural agricultural areas by providing subsidies to dairy and sheep farmers and setting quotas on many categories of agricultural imports (see Chapter III). Also, until this fisheries year, fishermen using small boats had been exempt from catch quotas: this exemption served to limit employment losses in rural towns that would result if many low-productivity small-scale fishing operations went out of business.

III.   Agriculture, resource management
and the environment

Iceland has only relatively lately developed a comprehensive environmental policy. Through the establishment of the Ministry for the Environment in February 1990, the responsibility for overall co-ordination of environmental policy was introduced at the level of government. Given its sparse population, modest level of industrialisation, availability of renewable energy resources and limited crop cultivation, problems of pollution have been rather insignificant. Building on this, the government has stated that its ''overall objective is that Iceland be, by the turn of the century, the cleanest country in the Western world and that an image of cleanliness and sustainability be associated with all sectoral and cross-sectoral developments''. However, the important environmental questions facing the nation pertain rather to natural resource issues such as the continued soil erosion and the degradation of the vegetative cover, influenced by harsh environmental conditions and agricultural developments, the quality of fisheries management and the exploitation of energy resources.

Icelandic agriculture: heavy intervention and environmental problems

Despite its severe climate[32], Iceland has always had a sizeable agricultural sector. It has been able to resist the inroads of historical increases in import availability only through recourse to a highly protectionist regime of government intervention and price support, especially in livestock products, which has been justified on zoo-sanitary grounds. This has proved to be increasingly costly over the years. Faced with economic stagnation since 1987 and the resulting budgetary pressures, the authorities have taken a hard look at their farm policies and begun to dismantle many of them with a view to reducing support and enhancing

45

farmers' market orientation. The first steps in this direction have only recently been implemented in the latest farm legislation. Although Iceland's offer in the Uruguay Round was to allow tarification of agricultural products, reduce tariffs on imported agricultural products by an average of 37 per cent and cut overall government support by 20 per cent[33], even after such liberalisation, Iceland's 5 200 full-time and part-time farmers will continue to benefit from one of the most heavily supported pricing and production systems in the OECD. This is in line with the main objectives of agricultural policies which continue to include self-sufficiency/food security and comparability of farmers' incomes with those of other workers (see the Act No. 99 of 1993 on the Production, Pricing and Sale of Agricultural Products). But farmers' future will depend increasingly on their capacity to reduce costs in order to meet inevitable increases in import competition and, probably, their ability to become an exporter of some niche-market products.

A brief description of the sector

In the late 1970s, Iceland had a larger agricultural sector, given the size of its economy, than most of the other high-income Members of the OECD. In 1977, it represented 5.2 per cent of total GDP (Table 12) and 9.0 per cent of all employment (Table 13). The ratio of the two indicates that farming was a low-productivity occupation, but an even larger differential is to be found in other countries. Of course, agriculture has been shrinking fairly steadily over time in virtually all Member countries. With strong overall economic growth and almost non-existent unemployment, that shrinkage was particularly marked in Iceland's case until about 1988, with a sharp slowdown in the trend thereafter in line with the stagnation that has marked recent economic performance. While new entry is undoubtedly extremely rare, many younger farmers are reluctant to leave the land because of their heavy debt loads taken on with a view to capital deepening. The result is that the average age of Icelandic farmers continues to rise, most recently reaching 52. Most farms operate on a very small scale, and sheep farming has for many become a secondary occupation. The average sheep farmer has only about 180 animals, while his dairy counterpart has only 19 cows. It is not uncommon for dairy farmers to have around 100 sheep.

Two products continue to make up well over half of all agricultural output by value: milk (about one-third) and sheepmeat (about one-quarter). Most of the

Table 12. **Gross value added in agriculture as percentage of GDP** [1]

	1977	1980	1985	1988	1989	1990
Iceland [2]	**5.2**	**5.0**	**4.5**	**3.0**	**3.0**	**2.7**
Canada	2.6	2.7	1.8	1.3	1.5	1.6
United States	2.8	2.6	2.0	1.6	1.8	1.8
Japan	3.5	2.5	2.3	1.9	1.9	1.9
Australia	4.0	4.8	3.5	4.0	3.7	2.9
New Zealand	8.9	9.4	6.4	5.9	6.2	5.4
Belgium	2.3	2.1	2.1	1.8	2.1	1.7
Denmark	4.6	4.1	4.2	3.3	3.7	3.5
France	4.2	3.7	3.4	2.8	2.9	2.8
Germany	2.2	1.6	1.4	1.3	1.3	1.1
Greece	14.0	14.7	14.4	13.0	13.2	11.6
Ireland	16.1	10.2	8.3	8.8	8.3	7.2
Italy	6.3	5.5	4.2	3.4	3.3	3.0
Luxembourg	2.6	2.1	2.2	1.8	1.9	1.7
Netherlands	4.0	3.4	4.0	3.9	4.3	4.1
Portugal	. .	7.3	5.9	4.1	4.2	4.1
Spain	7.3	6.0	5.3	4.7	4.2	4.0
United Kingdom	4.1	1.7	1.4	1.1	1.2	1.2
Austria	4.5	4.5	3.3	3.1	3.1	3.2
Finland	4.5	4.1	3.7	2.5	2.7	2.8
Norway	3.4	2.6	1.6	1.7	1.7	1.8
Sweden	1.8	1.4	1.2	1.0	1.0	0.9
Switzerland	3.1	2.8	2.6	2.3	. .	. .
Turkey	25.5	21.2	17.3	. .	. .	. .

1. At market prices.
2. At factor cost. Excludes imputed bank service charge.
Source: OECD (1993*d*) and Secretariat estimates based on submissions from the Icelandic authorities.

remainder is comprised of other livestock and products thereof; the only crops produced are dried hay and silage used as fodder, vegetables (primarily potatoes, tomatoes, cucumbers, carrots and cabbages) and flowers. Only 1.3 per cent of the island's land mass is cultivated. Exports of farm and food products (excluding fish) represent only a tiny share of total production and only slightly over 3 per cent of total merchandise exports; the majority of these exports is animal feed, in the form of fishmeal made from capelin. The real value of exports has been declining, for most categories since the mid-1980s. The only exception is fox and mink pelts – which expanded rapidly in the 1980s, only to retreat sharply in recent years amid mounting financial losses[34] – and live horses, for which exports quadrupled in the second half of the 1980s and have continued to rise since then,

Table 13. **Employment in agriculture as percentage of civilian employment**

	1977	1980	1985	1988	1989	1990	Average annual rate of change in per cent	
							1977-88	1988-90
Iceland [1]	**9.0**	**7.9**	**6.1**	**5.1**	**5.1**	**4.9**	**−5.0**	**−2.0**
Canada	5.7	5.4	5.1	4.5	4.3	4.2	−2.1	−3.4
United States	3.7	3.6	3.1	2.9	2.9	2.8	−2.2	−1.7
Japan	11.9	10.4	8.8	7.9	7.6	7.2	−3.7	−4.5
Australia	6.6	6.5	6.1	5.9	5.5	5.6	−1.0	−2.6
New Zealand	10.7	10.9	11.1	10.4	10.3	10.6	−0.3	+1.0
Belgium	3.5	3.2	3.1	2.8	2.8	2.7	−2.0	−1.8
Denmark	7.8	7.1	6.7	5.8	5.7	5.6	−2.7	−1.7
France	9.5	8.7	7.6	6.7	6.4	6.1	−3.1	−4.6
Germany	6.0	5.3	4.6	4.0	3.7	3.4	−3.6	−7.8
Greece	33.2	30.3	28.9	26.6	25.3	24.5	−2.0	−4.0
Ireland	21.3	18.3	15.9	15.4	15.1	15.0	−2.9	−1.3
Italy	15.8	14.3	11.2	9.9	9.3	9.0	−4.2	−4.7
Luxembourg	6.4	5.1	4.4	3.4	3.3	3.2	−5.6	−3.0
Netherlands	5.3	4.9	4.9	4.8	4.7	4.6	−0.9	−2.1
Portugal	32.9	27.3	23.9	20.7	19.0	17.8	−4.1	−7.3
Spain	21.1	19.3	18.3	14.4	13.0	11.8	−3.4	−9.5
United Kingdom	2.8	2.6	2.5	2.3	2.1	2.1	−1.8	−4.4
Austria	11.8	10.5	9.0	8.1	8.0	7.9	−3.4	−1.2
Finland	15.1	13.5	11.5	9.8	8.9	8.4	−3.9	−7.4
Norway	9.1	8.5	7.4	6.4	6.6	6.5	−3.1	+0.8
Sweden	6.1	5.6	4.8	3.8	3.6	3.3	−4.2	−6.8
Switzerland	7.6	6.9	6.1	5.7	5.6	5.6	−2.6	−0.9
Turkey	61.2	54.9	52.7	48.3	49.2	47.8	−2.1	−0.5

1. In full-time equivalents.
Source: OECD (1993*d*) and Secretariat estimates based on submissions from the Icelandic authorities.

reaching an estimated 2 400 animals in 1993. Imports too are a limited source of supply, making up only about one-quarter of apparent domestic consumption (but approximately half on a calorific basis) and 6 to 7 per cent of total merchandise imports. Vegetables, along with fruits and cereals, comprise the bulk of food products purchased from abroad. The only category for which there is any apparent direct import competition[35] is vegetables: here, a steady annual average of about 55 per cent of apparent consumption is provided by imports (but only during the seasons when domestic supply is inadequate). Virtually no unprocessed animal food products are imported.

Agricultural policies

As stated above, Iceland's farmers benefit from a substantial overall level of support and a complex system of intervention and regulatory control[36]. Four main aspects of this system are likely to lead to significant efficiency losses and social costs. First, there is an explicit goal of self-sufficiency in the import access regime: in general, imports are regarded as a residual source of supply and are therefore permitted only to the extent that domestic demand cannot be met from local production[37]. Imports of live animals and livestock products (including eggs and unpasteurised milk) are effectively banned on zoo-sanitary grounds[38], and domestic meat is freer from pharmaceutical products than almost any other in the world. Tariffs are levied on imported margarine and processed potatoes to protect those downstream sectors, and variable quotas are set on imports of flowers to protect domestic production. Because of the inefficiency of small-scale domestic production, the effect of the resulting autarkic outcome, in combination with the complex scheme of price regulation (see below) is to boost domestic food prices substantially above world prices (that is, the landed cost of imports, which would be the price of available world supplies plus a sizeable transport margin due to Iceland's small market and remote location), thereby reducing consumer welfare[39]. The relative price of food is higher than anywhere else in the OECD, apart from Turkey and Portugal (Diagram 8). Furthermore, such protection raises the equilibrium value of the real exchange rate, curbing the amount of diversification, so vital in a small and volatile economy such as Iceland's[40]. The only conceivable benefit derived from self-sufficiency is to enhance the security of food supplies, but, as Winters (1987) has argued, food is not really so special in terms of the risks to the population and "paying low prices usually and high prices occasionally dominates paying fairly high prices (resource costs) all the time" (p. 45).

A second major problem associated with the agricultural policy regime is its high budgetary cost. According to Ministry of Finance figures, total payments related to agriculture amounted to IKr 7.7 billion in 1993 (down from 10.7 billion in 1992), nearly 7 per cent of all Treasury expenditure and 2 per cent of GDP. About IKr 0.9 billion was paid to agricultural institutions such as the Land Reclamation Service, the Agricultural Research Institute and the Agricultural Colleges. Most of the remainder represents payments related to agricultural production[41], primarily subsidies which go mainly to milk and sheepmeat.

Diagram 8. **THE RELATIVE PRICE OF FOOD IN OECD COUNTRIES, 1990**[1]

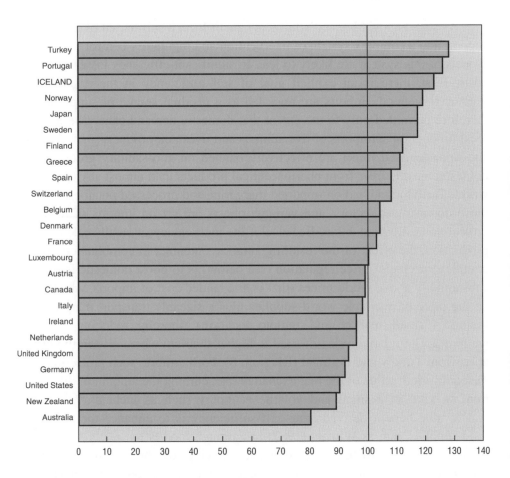

1. Price of final expenditure on food relative to price of GDP.
Source: OECD.

Besides outlays, the farm sector also benefits from an important tax expenditure: wages paid are subject to a social insurance levy (payroll tax) of only 3½ per cent, compared with the standard 6 per cent rate applied in most non-exporting sectors.

All these budgetary measures entail a fiscal burden which has to be financed either by heavier taxation or heavier borrowing[42]. If the payments are tax-financed, the principal macroeconomic effects, other than the price-distorting effects of subsidies (see below), are redistributive. But there are also costs of the added public administration and the excess burden/deadweight loss associated with the imposition of the tax (which some estimates put as high as 50 per cent of the proceeds of the tax). With deficit financing, there would be a resulting demand stimulus, with possibly greater inflationary pressures, unless the stimulus is completely offset by higher real interest rates, which would squeeze out interest-sensitive domestic spending. Such expenditure tends to be of a capital nature, and long-term growth rates could therefore be harmed. Higher demand pressure would also lead to greater import demand which, combined with the direct Treasury borrowing needs, would bring about an increase in foreign debt. The higher domestic interest rates and increased foreign borrowing would combine to put upward pressure on the exchange rate, crowding out price-sensitive net exports and worsening the current external deficit.

The production inefficiencies resulting from price distortions are the third main cost of current agricultural policies. This includes the inefficient allocation of resources between agriculture and other sectors, as well as that among different agricultural sectors themselves. Prices are supported and regulated at the producer level for sheepmeat, milk, eggs and poultry[43], and at the wholesale level as well for all but poultry. A so-called "six-person committee" (three each from the farmers' union and from labour organisations) set producer prices every three months based on total production costs, ostensibly taking into account changes in productivity. But calculations are based on the "average farm" for each commodity, maintaining inefficient production capacity, and there is less incentive to utilise best-practice technology in order to achieve static and dynamic efficiency. This system is up for renegotiation this year. Wholesale prices are determined by a separate "five-person committee" (two members each from the agricultural processing industry and the labour movement and one from the Office of Competition and Fair Trade). There are also ceilings on retail margins for certain dairy products and bulk sheepmeat. Until 1992, the State paid subsidies at the wholesale level up to a quota maximum, the amount of which was set in aggregate in a septennial contract between the government and the farmers union. If demand was insufficient to soak up available production, then the surplus[44] had to be dumped on world markets, necessitating export subsidies which peaked at IKr 2.4 billion (0.7 per cent of GDP) in 1991, the last year during which they were paid.

The upshot of this regulatory regime is that producer and wholesale prices in Iceland are among the highest in the OECD[45] (Table 14). Milk is perhaps the most conspicuous case: including direct payments (see below), Iceland's producer prices in 1992 were nearly six times those paid to farmers in New Zealand and some 40 per cent higher than in Japan, the Member country with the next highest price level. Although producer prices were cut in 1993, support remains substantial, with the advent of direct payments for milk, and little progress has been made by international standards in bringing down the real price over time. A similar situation prevails for sheepmeat: including direct payments, Icelandic producers are paid over 16 times what their Australian counterparts receive (for what is almost certainly a higher-quality product), more than anywhere else in the OECD except Switzerland. Downward real price adjustment through 1992 was also minimal in comparison with other OECD Member countries. Producer prices for beef are also relatively high by OECD standards – although only on a par with those found in other EFTA nations and well below Japanese levels – and the fall in real prices since 1991 has been substantial. Pigmeat producer prices in Iceland are easily the highest in the OECD, and again there has been very little change in real prices since 1984. Similarly, although there has been some drop in real prices since 1984, poultry prices remain far higher than anywhere else in the OECD, nearly seven times U.S. levels. Finally, egg prices in Iceland are also

Table 14. **Producer prices for farm products in Iceland**

US$/100 kg in 1993

	Iceland	Highest other OECD price		Lowest OECD price	
Milk	75.7	80.6	(Japan)	16.0	(New Zealand)
Sheepmeat	633.0	880.0	(Switzerland)	45.8	(Australia)
Beef	390.0	1 160.3	(Japan)	146.1	(New Zealand)
Pigmeat	548.0	369.3	(Japan)	127.2	(Canada)
Poultry	444.6	341.8	(Switzerland)	79.1	(United States)
Eggs	362.4	426.5	(Switzerland)	90.2	(United States)

Note: Cross-country comparisons are problematic to the extent that there may be international quality differences.
Source: Annex tables 1-6.

52

extremely high (over five times U.S. levels), although lower than in Switzerland; real price declines over the past five years have been meagre.

In April 1991, the government and the farmers agreed that, beginning in September 1992, subsidies at the wholesale level would be replaced with direct payments (the government has guaranteed payment of 50 per cent of the producer price of sheepmeat and 47.1 per cent for milk), leaving farmers and the food processing industry responsible for production and marketing. Note that the direct payments are only partly decoupled from production, as payments are sensitive to variations in production around quota levels. The hope was to adjust domestic production of sheepmeat and milk to declining domestic demand[46], to lower consumer prices of these products (real prices of sheepmeat and milk are to be cut by 20 and 14 per cent by 1998, respectively) and to cut government outlays over the medium term[47]. In the short term, however, outlays were boosted, because farmers were compensated for quota reductions, even if compensation was not adequate to bring about these reductions voluntarily. Furthermore, efficiency may have been at least temporarily damaged: while sheepmeat quota and production have been slashed by nearly a third thus far, the number of producers has fallen only 15 to 16 per cent due, no doubt, to the weakness in the labour market. In general, such direct payments may indeed shift the burden of support away from consumers, and, to the extent that they are quite invariant to production levels, they are more effective than subsidies and other forms of market price support in terms of transfer efficiency (OECD, 1993c) – given the officially-declared objective to maintain farmers' incomes at a level corresponding to those of other working occupations.

Levies on inputs and outputs are another potential source of market distortion. There are output levies – differentiated by product – to fund various farmers organisations as well as the the Agricultural Production Board; to finance investment subsidies to producers of agricultural products and, to a lesser extent, to processing plants (a total of nearly 1 billion kronur in 1992, with a total outstanding of nearly IKr 9 billion); to provide natural disaster relief and assistance; to equalise the cost of operating dairies across the island (in order to enable the dairies to pay the same price for milk to all farmers)[48]; and to assist in pricing different dairy products according to relative demands. Imported feed is subject to a levy which is currently set at 67 per cent but was as high as 200 per cent in the early 1980s[49]; most of this is refunded to livestock and product producers, but about one-sixth goes to the Treasury. Consideration is being given to abolishing this levy.

The overall level of support has therefore been considerable, and even if it has declined somewhat since 1991, it remains one of the highest in the OECD and is nearly double the OECD average. The OECD's Directorate for Food, Agriculture and Fisheries has not yet produced PSEs/CSEs (that is, producer and consumer subsidy equivalents – PSEs and CSEs)[50] for Iceland but is preparing a major review of Icelandic agricultural policies during 1994 which will include PSE/CSE calculations, prepared on the basis of the established methodology applied to other Member countries. Estimates made by the Icelandic government, which have not yet been examined in detail by the OECD, show support in 1988 of IKr 9.0 billion (Table 15)[51]. Since then, support has declined fairly steadily in real terms, but so has the value of production; until 1991, the ratio of the two remained largely unchanged, after having increased during the mid-1980s, especially for sheepmeat (Diagram 9). It was only in 1992 and 1993 that the percentage PSE fell – from a 1991 peak of 87.6 per cent to 75.7 per cent in 1993. About half the decline is attributable to the larger decline in market support than the increase in direct payments, while the other half is the result of changing input costs and reduced provision of general services. Nevertheless, Iceland remains among the OECD Member nations which provide the most support to their farmers (Diagram 10). Product-specific PSEs have not been calculated, but the market-price-support component (that is, excluding direct payments) of the PSEs is the highest for poultry and eggs and the lowest for sheepmeat[52]. Thus, merely by reducing the dispersion of assistance, there would be a marginal gain in allocative efficiency.

A fourth inefficiency associated with Iceland's agricultural policies is the negative externality imposed on the environment. Even though the situation has improved significantly, artificial stimulation of agricultural production through import bans and price subsidisation has meant a greater risk of environmental degradation. While the cultivation of crops is minimal in Iceland, and therefore there is little problem with groundwater pollution from nitrogenous fertiliser run-off[53], there has been a long-term problem of soil erosion[54]. This has been due primarily to the harsh climatic conditions, but also, in part, to wetlands drainage (1 200 to 1 400 square kilometres this century) and the overgrazing of livestock (constrained until this century by the lack of winter feed), especially in sensitive

Table 15. **Preliminary PSE calculations**

IKr million

	1988	1989	1990	1991	1992	1993
Market support						
Total	7 358.7	8 625.4	9 650.7	10 303.5	7 714.6	4 674.6
Direct payments						
Subsidies on wool	148.8	164.0	163.3	155.8	276.6	250.0
Refund of levies	321.0	392.1	254.5	348.6	285.0	285.0
Direct payments for sheepmeat					1 764.0	1 672.2
Direct payments for milk						2 477.0
Total	469.8	556.1	417.8	504.4	2 325.6	4 684.2
Reduction of production costs						
Contributions according to laws						
on cultivation	172.1	203.7	160.6	302.1	212.3	107.5
State-farm fund	14.9	11.8	14.2	25.9	5.3	0.0
Feed levies	−248.0	−313.5	−152.2	−69.5	−75.8	−80.0
Total	−61.0	−98.0	22.6	258.5	141.8	27.5
General services						
Contributions according to laws						
on animal breeding	26.4	19.1	16.8	23.1	26.1	74.9
Agricultural Society	66.6	73.7	77.0	81.5	107.6	82.0
Agricultural Productivity Fund	429.0	490.0	591.7	666.4	340.0	250.0
Agricultural Investment Fund	34.6	38.8	47.4	53.7	0.0	0.0
Veterinary services	43.6	45.6	51.9	54.7	54.5	60.3
Farmers pension fund	275.8	260.0	280.0	255.0	270.0	185.0
Appraisal of agricultural products	4.8	5.1	−4.1	0.0	0.0	0.0
Disease prevention (sheep)	277.0	420.3	321.2	326.3	192.9	132.7
Quarantine station (cattle)	5.0	4.9	8.3	7.8	6.3	0.0
Price administration committees	6.0	6.6	6.3	6.9	7.0	7.3
Agricultural Research Institute	93.0	95.1	115.4	132.2	134.3	117.3
Miscellaneous	5.6	26.6	9.1	12.8	1.6	1.0
Total	1 267.4	1 485.8	1 521.0	1 620.4	1 140.3	910.5
Total PSE	9 034.9	10 569.3	11 612.1	12 686.8	11 322.3	10 296.8
Percentage PSE	86.7	85.7	85.8	87.6	82.7	75.7

Source: Preliminary data provided by the Ministry of Agriculture, October 1993.

areas (there are no limits on where sheep may graze, because the right of access is virtually unlimited in Iceland). Since the settlement of the island in the year 874, destruction of the vegetative cover has been severe (Diagram 11), due to the erosive nature of the soil – half of the initial soil and plant cover has been lost. For example, forest coverage of the island has declined to a mere 3 000 hect-

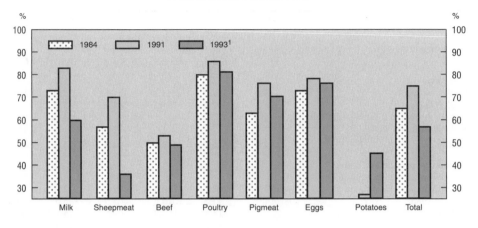

Diagram 9. **MARKET PRICE SUPPORT SINCE 1984**

In per cent of production value

1984   1991   1993[1]

Milk   Sheepmeat   Beef   Poultry   Pigmeat   Eggs   Potatoes   Total

1. If direct payments for milk and sheepmeat are included, the corresponding figures for 1993 would be 125 and 175, respectively, while the grand total would be 107 per cent.
Source: OECD calculations based on preliminary data provided by the Ministry of Agriculture, October 1993.

ares out of some 2¹/₂ million, and a considerable portion of these woodlands as well as a large majority of the highlands is considered to be in poor condition[55]. Even if the numbers of most livestock species have fallen off (the number of sheep peaked at 891 000 in 1978, but by 1992 they had fallen to 487 000 – possibly a sustainable level), there has been a marked increase in the number of horses (from 30 000 in 1960 to 74 000 in 1991), and they impose much greater damage per animal than other domestic animals – by some estimates as much as ten times as much[56].

Both the authorities and the people of Iceland are now well aware of the soil erosion problem, although its exact extent remains unknown and only recently has there been any progress, albeit minimal, in integrating environmental concerns into agricultural policy. Volunteer tree planting and seeding programmes involved more than 8 000 people and succeeded in planting 3.4 million trees in 1990. In 1991, the government adopted a National Soil Conservation Strategy with a view to achieving sustainable land use. Its environmental strategy document (Ministry for the Environment, 1993) calls for soil erosion to be brought

Diagram 10. **PRODUCER SUBSIDY EQUIVALENTS: AN INTERNATIONAL COMPARISON**[1]

In per cent

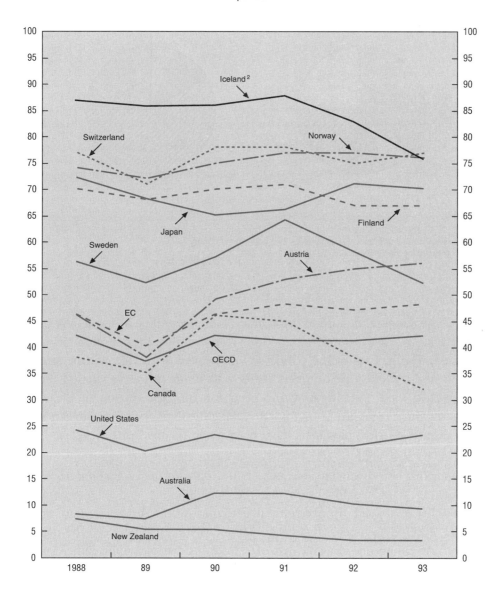

1. 1992 data are estimates and 1993 data are provisional.
2. Based on preliminary data provided by the Ministry of Agriculture, October 1993.
Source: OECD.

Diagram 11. **REDUCTION IN VEGETATIVE COVER**

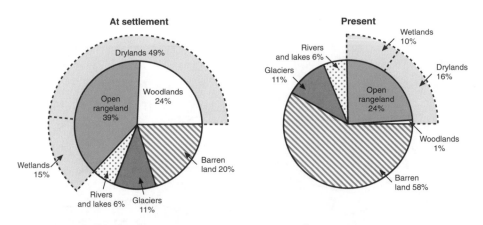

Note: Very recent research based on satellite images suggests that the present share of "open rangeland" may amount to 42 per cent and "barren land" may be much less than the Diagram shows. These figures are controversial due to differences in terminology and definition of concepts.
Source: Ministry for the Environment (1992).

under control before the turn of the century. Grazing will be allowed only in non-sensitive areas. Also, landowner and user responsibility for conservation will be increased. The powers of the public soil conservation service will be strengthened; it already subsidises farmers' efforts to improve the vegetation on their land, with a view to mitigating the need for summer grazing in the central highlands. But a legal provision for subsidising the drainage of wetlands is still in force, even if no such payments have been made for the last few years.

The overall goal should be to incorporate the social opportunity cost of environmental improvement and degradation into the individual farmer's decision-making. This would ensure that the contemporary and inter-generational externalities generated by agricultural activities would be taken into account (OECD, 1993a). In theory, the system should distinguish between the marginal cost of preventing erosion and that of reclaiming barren public land. And this cost should be set against the marginal value of extending vegetation cover. If the latter could be quantified, then it would be desirable to institute a bounty per hectare reclaimed, offset by a grazing fee per animal in the commons: this would be in conformity with the polluter pays principle[57]. Soil conservation benefits would also accrue to the nation if producer prices for livestock and related products were moved toward international levels, thereby reducing intensity. Such agricultural policy reforms would contribute to the generation of a variety of favourable environmental effects (OECD, 1994) and would thereby serve to put Icelandic agriculture on a more sustainable footing.

Energy resources and other environmental questions

Virtually all energy production is from renewable, essentially non-polluting hydroelectric and geothermal sources. Imported oil and coal make up less than a third of total primary energy supply, down from over half in the early 1970s. Other than in industry, substitution possibilities are thought now to be largely exhausted, but the authorities intend to favour hydro and geothermal power use in industry through differential pricing and taxation. Engineering estimates point to a possibility of generating 64 000 GWh/year of hydro power and 190 000 of geothermal power. However, cost considerations preclude the development of most of this resource, leaving an economically feasible potential of 30 000 GWh/year of hydro and 20 000 GWh/year of geothermal. To this point only about one tenth has been developed, leaving an unexploited potential equal to $^3/_4$ of a per cent of the total amount of energy consumed in the OECD. To exploit this potential would, however, have some environmental impact mainly because of large structures, dams and distribution systems which exclude alternative land use and alter the beauty of the landscape. Existing energy-intensive industry has relied heavily on the availability of cheap power, first hydroelectric (initially for the production of fertiliser and cement and later for aluminium and ferro-silicon) and then geothermal (diatomite, seasalt and seaweed drying). The prospects are that additional energy development will eventually take place to provide for the needs for energy-intensive industry: another aluminium smelter will probably be built as soon as world-wide demand recovers, and technology for long-distance undersea cables is now sufficiently advanced that Icelandic power may soon be a potential source of clean energy to Western European users.

Despite exhibiting an energy intensity which is the highest in the OECD, Iceland's air quality is very high due to its isolated location, low population density and minimal reliance on fossil fuels. However, some long-range transport of persistent pollutants from Europe and North America does occur, and local air pollution problems, mainly due to motor vehicle emissions, have occasionally developed. Fishmeal factories and metal smelters are the main industrial sources of pollution, while waste incineration by open fires generates pollution in a few areas. The harnessing of geothermal power does pose localised problems (sulphur), and suspended dust concentrations due to soil erosion can be high. Emissions of sulphur dioxide into the atmosphere are lower than the OECD average (Table 16), but a further substantial amount of sulphur (H2S) is released with the harnessing of geothermal power. Emissions of nitrogen oxides are the highest in the OECD, both on a per capita and per unit of GDP basis. This is attributable in no small part to the fuel combustion of the large fishing fleet. The fleet is also responsible for about a quarter of all carbon dioxide emissions, with manufacturing the source of another quarter; but these remain moderate by international standards, nearly a third below OECD averages on a per capita basis. At 2.8 tonnes per person per year, emissions of other greenhouse gases are, however, considerable. Three-quarters of such emissions are from industrial sources. CFC use has been cut by 70 per cent since 1986 and will be eliminated entirely by 1995, in advance of the requirements of the Montreal Protocol. The

Table 16. **Selected environmental data: an Iceland-OECD comparison**[1]

	Kg per capita		Kg per 1 000 US\$ GDP[2]	
	Iceland	OECD	Iceland	OECD
Air pollution				
Emissions of sulphur oxides	25.8	51.7	1.9	3.7
Emissions of nitrogen oxides	105.4	43.3	7.6	3.1
Emissions of carbon dioxide	8 600	12 100	620	860
Solid waste generation				
Industrial waste	735	1 708	53	122
Municipal waste	314	509	23	36

	Iceland	OECD
Water usage and treatment		
Per capita water withdrawal, cubic metres	411	1 100
Per cent of population served by public waste water treatment	6	62

1. In most cases, data refer to 1990 and include eastern Germany.
2. At 1985 prices and purchasing power parities.
Source: OECD (1993*b*) and updates.

problem of lead in the atmosphere is in the process of being solved: lead levels have fallen in line with the decline in the lead content of motor fuels. Imports of lead-free petrol began in 1988 and its consumption reached 80 per cent of the market by 1993; also, there has been a requirement for three-way catalytic converters or equivalent pollution-control equipment on all petrol-driven passenger cars imported since 1 July 1992. Finally, very little atmospheric radioactivity is present in Iceland.

Waste management is largely a responsibility of the local authorities. At present far less solid waste is generated in Iceland than in the average OECD country on a per capita basis and in relation to GDP (Table 16 above). But only 10-12 per cent is recycled or prepared for recycling abroad – in part due to the small size of the island and the dispersed population – and about 40 per cent is disposed of in what the authorities term ''an unsatisfactory manner''. The government intends to spur the local authorities to deal with all solid waste satisfactorily by the end of 1995 and to cut the generation of waste by half by the end of the decade. Recycling has been assisted by a deposit scheme on beverage containers which was put in place in 1989; this programme has achieved a return rate of around 73 per cent. Fees are also levied on plastic shopping bags, with half the proceeds going to the interest group, the Environmental Union. Incentives for businesses to reduce their waste are provided by charging for removal on the basis of weight, but households pay a flat fee. Only businesses are required to separate their waste. Two thirds of solid waste is disposed of in landfills, and the remainder is burnt in open fires (15 per cent) or in one of three incineration plants (6 per cent), none of which is as yet equipped with satisfactory pollution controls. While a modern facility to handle solid wastes now exists in Reykjavik, serving about 60 per cent of the population, it might take up to one billion kronur in investment outlays to bring the rest of the country up to these standards. Proposed legislation would impose fees on the handling of scrap metal and deposits on motor vehicles to ensure their proper disposal. Hazardous waste has been collected only since 1990, with a return rate of around some 30 per cent in recent years. The government's objective is for all communities to have systems in place for collection and safe disposal of hazardous waste before 1995.

Waste water is virtually entirely discharged into the ocean untreated: only 6 per cent of the population is served by treatment plants, the lowest proportion in the OECD, except Turkey. Conditions in the coastal zone, where effective mixing of deep-sea and coastal water takes place, are very favourable for receiving domestic sewage from primary treatment facilities. Eutrophication has not been observed anywhere in this zone. Municipalities in the capital area have joined forces to treat effluent[58]. The resulting project, which is to be finished by 1998, is estimated to cost some IKr 5 billion. In the outlying regions, where costs are higher, another 2 to 4 billion kronur might be required. The national government believes all communities should plan to improve their sewage systems by 1995. Freshwater resources are, however, abundant and of high quality. As a result Iceland has recently developed a small bottled water export industry, and a major expansion in aquaculture occurred in the late 1980s[59]. While recent data show that per capita water withdrawal is well below both OECD and OECD Europe averages, demands could surge if the fish farming industry (an intensive user) is further developed. But with less than 100 million cubic metres of water withdrawn per year out of an estimated 16 billion available annually, it is extremely unlikely that any pressures on capacity will develop.

But another growing sector, the tourism industry, could put pressure on water resources and the environment more generally. To the degree that Iceland is chosen as a tourist destination because of the quality of its environment, future growth prospects will depend on balancing the needs of visitors and the longer-term maintenance of the natural resource base. Accordingly, Iceland has been steadily expanding the share of its territory which is protected and conserved – from 0.5 per cent in 1970 to 7.7 per cent in 1980 and 9.0 per cent in 1990, compared with an OECD average figure of 7.7 per cent. But this may still not be sufficient owing to the spread of tourist and recreational activities beyond their traditional areas and to problems resulting from poorly defined property rights in uninhabited areas. Thus, the OECD's recent environmental performance review of Iceland (OECD, 1993b) recommended that a target be set for protected and conserved areas of 15 per cent of the national territory before the end of the decade. Consideration is being given to making private firms responsible for individual sites, leaving them free to meet environmental requirements in a cost-minimising way. This will probably shift a share of the burden of nature conservation onto tourists as ultimate users.

The authorities have been increasing their spending for the environment ever since the Ministry for the Environment was established in 1990 (Table 17)[60]. Approximately 2 per cent of Treasury outlays have an environment-related objec-

Table 17. **Gross environment-related public expenditure**

IKr million

	1991 Actual	1992 Actual	1993 Budget	1994 Budget
Ministry for the Environment	97.1	123.6	138.2	134.3
Nature conservation	125.1	116.5	112.1	105.7
Physical planning, geodetic survey	224.5	254.5	249.8	228.9
Meteorological research	292.7	284.2	284.6	293.2
Wildlife management	132.2	163.1	107.5	105.0
Marine pollution	13.3	20.3	21.1	17.2
Air pollution, hazardous materials	94.6	90.7	93.0	96.0
Soil conservation [1]	318.4	330.3	218.0	206.1
Forestry [1]	280.7	339.0	277.5	270.7
Marine research	597.4	648.2	623.8	624.3
Total	2 176.2	2 370.2	2 125.6	2 081.4
Percentage of outlays	1.7	1.9	1.8	1.8

1. Net figures for soil conservation are IKr 218, 240, 202 and 196 million, respectively. Net figures for forestry are IKr 181, 203, 212 and 208 million, respectively.
Source: Ministry of Finance and Ministry for the Environment.

tive. By far the most important component is for marine research, but meteorological research, afforestation and soil conservation efforts are also significant. For 1994, however, budgetary stringency has forced a virtual freeze in expenditure, as it has in other domains.

The European Economic Area (EEA) agreement has some important implications for environmental policies: 38 EC directives are being adopted, of which 32 are binding. Some were dealt with in anticipation: a bill obliging the government to provide environmental information was passed in March 1993, and another requiring environmental impact assessments was approved in May 1993 to take effect a year later. All the others will come into effect by the beginning of 1995. The assessment law may be used to integrate environmental considerations into agricultural policies, thereby confronting the problem of subsidising wetlands drainage (see above).

Other medium-term environmental goals of the government have been outlined in a recent Strategy document (Ministry for the Environment, 1993). These will be developed in an action plan to be prepared by mid-1994 under the supervision of the Ministry for the Environment on the basis of reports by seven task forces with broad-based membership. Four basic principles underpin the Strategy: *i)* the public has a right to information and to participate in decision-making; *ii)* activities which might possibly cause serious environmental damage should be prohibited until the contrary can be proven (the ''precautionary approach''); *iii)* polluters should pay for the environmental degradation they cause (including paying for impact assessments and monitoring); and *iv)* those who utilise natural resources should pay for their conservation and management. Finally, an environmental protection act is in preparation, and the constitution is to be revised to make explicit the right of all present and future generations to a healthy environment.

The marine environment and fisheries management

Iceland's marine environment is crucial to the country's well-being, since economic outcomes depend so heavily on the fisheries[61]. Fortunately, the waters around Iceland are largely unpolluted, and the nation's marine exports have retained their reputation for the highest quality. Although waste water remains untreated in many coastal areas outside of Reykjavik, the population is so small, and currents brisk, that build-up of algae from sewage and phosphates is minimal. In a few areas sewage and aquaculture releases have created a minor aesthetic blemish, but no health problems. Likewise there is little problem with pollution from trace metals accumulating in the fish stock. Of all the common trace metals, only cadmium appears in the cod stock in noticeable quantities, and even that is far below levels considered dangerous (Ministry for the Environment, 1992). Traces of polychlorinated biphenyls (PCBs) have been found in cod livers, but at much lower levels than in cod fished from the North Sea[62]. There has been minor pollution from drifting materials accumulating at certain points on the north-west coast, where ocean currents converge. Packaging materials and sections of lost or cut-off nets are the most common examples. The law no longer permits fishing vessels to throw their solid waste overboard, and significant improvements have been made in garbage collection from ships in harbours.

The government has also taken steps to limit pollution from fuel use by the fishing fleet. About 4 per cent of the fleet's energy use occurs in harbour or dry-dock, and in these areas the price of electricity to the fleet has been cut to discourage use of diesel fuel when docked, with a view to limiting emissions of nitrous oxides and other greenhouse gases. However, despite government efforts to encourage fossil-fuel conservation by the fleet, its oil consumption has not fallen over the past decade or so, since the trend toward trawling has led to greater energy use per tonne of catch than fishing using other methods.

Given its small population, most of the risk to Iceland's marine environment comes from transnational sources. Accumulated pollutants may be carried by sea or through the atmosphere from other countries by prevailing winds and ocean currents. The government is therefore concerned about the risk of sea-borne radioactivity due to present and future emissions from operation of the Sellafield nuclear reprocessing facility in north-west England[63]. The government has also taken steps to establish emergency preparedness and response capacity to handle marine environmental disasters such as oil spills at all major Icelandic ports by 1995 (Ministry for the Environment, 1993). However, at this point marine pollution control is not a major issue: the key marine environmental question is fisheries management.

Fisheries management issues

One of the most difficult tasks for the government has been to maximise long-run net revenues from the nation's primary natural resource: the stock of cod and other fish in Icelandic waters. Unmanaged competition would not be the best means to this end, since individual fishing firms would not pay the entire social cost of their use of the common resource. The catch of an individual fishing operation in a given year would have negligible impact on that same firm's catch and earnings in future years; in total, however, catch levels beyond a certain point are unsustainable and can eventually lead to a collapse of fish stocks and long-run fisheries revenues. Such a disaster occurred to Iceland's herring fisheries in the late 1960s. The result was an attempt by the authorities to gain control over the fisheries in the 1970s through the extension of the fishing limit zone from 12 miles to 50 miles in 1972 and to 200 miles in 1975, in line with international treaties. A similar catastrophic situation is now facing the North American cod fisheries, and cod stocks are also low in the North Sea and the Irish Sea. Since 1977, the government has tried to deal with such external costs of fishing by setting quotas on key species – until 1984, through a system of ''effort quotas'' and thereafter of quotas for the allowable catch of most types of fish (see below). The present regime, dating back to 1991, is the fifth version of the quota system, but it is likely to prove much more effective than its predecessors. The quota system is supplemented by technical measures to conserve stocks: nets are subject to minimum mesh sizes, and some fishing locations and/or equipment are forbidden in order to protect spawning grounds and juvenile fish. Finally, an annual licence is required to fish in Icelandic waters, and entry of new vessels must be preceded by removal of a vessel or vessels with similar capacity.

Each spring the Marine Research Institute (MRI) estimates a maximum safe catch for the major fish species, and since 1984 the Fisheries Ministry has set quotas based on these MRI recommendations – the "total allowable catch" (TAC). For many species, the MRI recommendations have been followed reasonably closely (Diagram 12). The glaring exceptions are cod, by far the most important species for fishery earnings, and, to a lesser extent, redfish, greenland halibut and saithe. For these species, the government's catch quotas have consistently exceeded MRI recommendations, and quota loopholes (see below) have made the actual cod catch larger than the government's announced catch quota. Since the inception of MRI recommendations (1976), the actual (cod) catch has exceeded those recommendations by an average of 22 per cent; 1992/93 was no exception with a gap of 24 per cent. This overfishing, combined with unfavourable environmental conditions, has led to a sharp decline in the fishable stock of cod, and a crisis in the fisheries[64].

The MRI has thus warned that without significant cuts in the cod catch from 1992/93 levels, the cod stock in Icelandic waters might well collapse within the next few years. Estimates of the spawning stock biomass have fallen sharply since measurement began in 1955 and are still close to the lowest on record[65]. For the 1993/94 fisheries year, the government has again cut cod quotas: the targeted catch is about 25 per cent smaller than the 1992/93 catch, and almost 50 per cent below the actual 1990 catch. However, the MRI had recommended even greater stringency: the government's target exceeded the MRI recommendation by about 10 per cent[66]. Thus, some long-run risk remains of a collapse in cod stocks. A 1993 government study estimates this risk to be of the order of 7 per cent if the actual cod catch were to continue for the next few years at the government's 1993/1994 target levels (Baldursson *et al.*, 1993). However, stocks were deemed more likely to recover gradually over the coming decade; in this more probable scenario, sustainable cod production would ultimately reach levels about twice the 1993/94 target catch. Following near-term retrenchment, long-run prospects

Diagram 12. FISHERIES MANAGEMENT: LANDINGS VERSUS RECOMMENDED CATCH

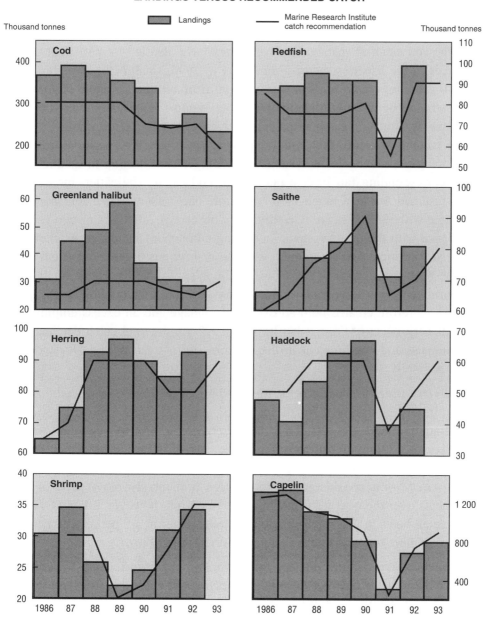

Thousand tonnes

Landings

Marine Research Institute catch recommendation

Thousand tonnes

Source: Marine Research Institute (1993).

for gross fisheries revenues may therefore be more encouraging, despite earlier lapses in fisheries management.

To this point, not only have government quota-setting procedures failed to keep the cod catch at sustainable levels, they have also led to inefficient use of resources in the fisheries sector. From 1984 to 1990, small boats (weighing less than 10 gross registered tonnes) were exempt from all quotas, while larger boats had to choose between two alternative quota systems. Their choice lay between catch quotas (limits on catch tonnage in a given year) and ''effort quotas'' (limits on the amount of effort, that is days spent at sea fishing)[67]. The initial result of introducing the management system was a 21 per cent decline in fishing effort and a corresponding fall in cost per unit of cod catch. Thereafter, increases in effort resumed but at a much more moderate pace (about 2 per cent per year, compared with the 6 per cent rate previously observed). After one or two years of experience with the quota system, increasing numbers of fishing firms chose the effort-quota option, and since there were no restrictions on entry of small boats into the fleet, the number of these boats ballooned (Table 18). These small boats are more labour-intensive than the larger trawlers, and this loophole in the quota system[68] therefore created both an excess of tonnage and an excess employment in the fisheries sector. From 1984 through 1992/93, the total catch declined, but fleet tonnage and employment in the fisheries did not fall until 1992, and then only marginally.

Given current low cod stocks, more fishing effort has been needed to attain quotas: in this environment, small boats are typically at only a modest disadvantage relative to large trawlers. Thus for current needs, fleet tonnage may be only 10-20 per cent too high. Furthermore, in the current recession fishermen thrown out of work by restructuring of the fleet might well have difficulty finding new employment[69] – a consideration arguing for a relatively slow pace of boat retirements over the next year or two. In the long run, however, a larger fraction of the small boats in the fleet is likely to be redundant: in all, perhaps 30 per cent or more of fleet tonnage could be retired (Gylfason, 1990).

Much of the fishing industry has for many years lacked the incentive to produce the targeted catch efficiently – excess labour and capital has not left the sector. A first attempt at creating incentives for rationalisation was made in 1984, when limited trading of quotas was introduced. Fisheries firms – but not fish processing firms without boats[70] – could buy the right to catch a certain fraction

Table 18. Size of the fishing fleet, 1970-92

| | Number of fishing vessels[1] | | | | | | Gross registered tonnages (GRT) | | | | | |
| | Total | of which: | | | | | Total | of which: | | | | |
		0-12 GRT	13-24 GRT	25-99 GRT	100-499 GRT	> 500 GRT		0-12 GRT	13-24 GRT	25-99 GRT	100-499 GRT	> 500 GRT
1970	766	207	84	256	218	11	76 060	1 729	1 153	14 494	42 048	16 636
1975	910	267	87	255	281	20	97 383	2 356	1 196	14 294	57 413	22 134
1980	874	266	85	218	266	39	108 971	2 264	1 522	12 043	64 078	29 064
1981	846	255	75	202	274	40	111 029	2 230	1 281	10 994	66 890	29 634
1982	841	252	74	191	284	40	113 583	2 141	1 292	10 285	70 231	29 634
1983	833	252	71	185	285	40	113 672	2 096	1 262	9 911	79 800	20 603
1984	830	252	70	182	286	40	114 142	2 087	1 253	9 789	80 410	20 603
1985	826	250	70	181	285	40	113 580	2 065	1 255	9 738	70 982	29 540
1986	820	254	67	171	288	40	113 678	2 104	1 208	9 080	71 686	29 600
1987	901	326	68	169	294	44	118 202	2 671	1 242	8 990	72 423	32 876
1988	955	379	70	166	294	46	120 321	3 109	1 275	8 830	72 529	34 578
1989	964	395	69	159	293	48	121 110	3 255	1 262	8 452	71 936	36 205
1990	997	445	64	148	292	48	120 400	3 615	1 158	7 739	71 729	36 159
1991	996	438	68	147	294	49	121 708	3 506	1 209	7 699	72 515	36 779
1992	953	427	66	136	281	43	120 397	3 333	1 162	7 045	74 007	34 850

1. Excluding open boats.
Source: National Economic Institute.

of the industry-wide catch quota for the year ("year quota"). In principle, availability of this trading system should have encouraged the most efficient firms to buy quota rights and the least efficient firms to sell them and leave the business. However, more than a third of the catch was subject to effort quotas rather than catch quotas in the 1980s, and those effort quotas could not be traded. Thus, only in 1991, when virtually all of fleet tonnage became subject to catch quotas, did the trade in quotas really take off (Table 19) – and in the past fisheries year, about two-thirds of the year's quota for groundfish was traded. Equally important, starting in 1991 fisheries firms were permitted to buy "permanent quota" – the right to catch a fraction of each year's overall catch quota in perpetuity. Permanent-quota trading has risen in the past three years to about 13 per cent of the total allowable catch for cod[71]. The number of vessels in the fleet declined about 4 per cent in 1992, and permanent-quota trading may have contributed to the rationalisation, although two other considerations were also very important, as discussed below.

Quota reductions and excess capacity have contributed to poor profitability for the fisheries since 1988 (Table 20). It is quite striking, though, that the worst performance has been by boats and small trawlers, which have steadily lost money, while the larger trawlers, in particular freezer trawlers, have been consistently profitable. Poor profit performance might have been expected to induce small fishing firms to leave the business, especially in light of the heavy leverage

Table 19. **Transfers of quota between vessels, 1984-92/93**

As a percentage of total groundfish catch[1]

Transfer[2]	1984	1985	1986	1987	1988	1989	1990	1991[3]	1991-92[4]	1992-93
Type A	4.2	3.3	2.6	1.8	4.0	5.1	5.5	12.2	18.7	24.6
Type B	3.8	3.4	2.2	1.9	3.1	3.7	3.6	9.0	8.8	12.2
Type C	1.1	1.7	1.1	0.1	2.4	2.7	1.7	4.3	5.3	8.1
Type D	3.6	5.8	2.7	2.2	4.7	4.4	6.9	7.8	13.5	21.6
Total	12.6	14.2	8.5	6.0	14.3	16.0	17.8	33.4	46.3	66.5

1. These groundfish quotas are measured in kilograms of cod equivalents and represent temporary "year-quota" transfers only.
2. Type A: Transfers between vessels with the same owner.
   Type B: Transfers between vessels with different owners operated from the same port.
   Type C: Offsetting transfers of different species with equal value between vessels with different owners.
   Type D: Transfers between vessels with different owners operated from different ports.
3. First eight months of 1991.
4. September to August fisheries year.
Source: Ministry of Fisheries and National Economic Institute.

Table 20. **Profitability of demersal fisheries, 1983-93**

Per cent of gross income

	1984	1985	1986	1987	1988	1989	1990	1991	1992	Sept. 1993
Net profits [1]										
Fishing, total	−9.4	−3.8	2.1	1.3	−1.5	−1.8	3.0	2.2	2.9	−3.0
Trawlers										
less than 500 GRT	−10.5	−3.9	4.1	5.3	3.6	−2.0	−2.2	0.6	−1.5	−9.7
Trawlers										
larger than 500 GRT	−6.7	−1.1	4.9	7.1	6.1	4.3	9.7	6.1	9.8	−1.6
Boats	−8.6	−4.3	−0.7	−4.1	−8.1	−5.5	−1.1	−2.0	2.1	−5.1
Freezer trawlers	4.9	10.2	11.1	9.8	8.8					
Fish processing, total [2]	−7.4	−2.6	3.9	3.6	−6.7	−5.6	1.7	2.7	−3.5	−0.1
Freezing plants	−6.6	−3.4	0.4	0.5	−7.8	−1.7	3.9	4.1	−1.9	4.7
Saltfish processing	−13.0	−0.1	10.9	8.7	−5.3	−11.7	−2.9	0.2	−6.8	−13.6

1. Gross profits less imputed cost of capital, *i.e.* interest payments and depreciation.
2. With payments into the Price Equalization Fund added to income and payments out of the Fund subtracted from income.
Source: National Economic Institute.

of most fishing firms' finances[72]. But in a recessionary environment with rising joblessness many of the fishermen in these money-losing small operations have no other source of employment. However, increasing numbers of mergers and bankruptcies have forced the issue in the past year or so, leading to a reduction in fleet size and increased unemployment among fishermen in some of the smaller towns. With sharply reduced cod quotas in 1993/94, fisheries bankruptcies are likely to be more widespread for at least another year.

Finally, since January 1991 the government has operated a Fisheries Rationalisation Fund[73], through which a subsidy is paid to owners who retire their boats. However, the subsidy – 30 per cent of the insurance value of the vessel – has apparently been insufficient to attract many retirements, and little in the way of rationalisation has resulted (1.3 per cent of capacity in 1992). Late in 1992 the government announced its intention to raise the subsidy to 45 per cent in the hope of increasing annual retirements to 3 per cent of capacity, but enabling legislation is still before the Parliament.

Over the medium term the government hopes to encourage further retirement of small boats and older trawlers, thereby boosting productivity and profitability in the industry, through a proposed Fisheries Development Fund: a bill to create this fund is scheduled to be introduced in Parliament over the next few months. The Fund would take over the functions and assets of the Rationalisation Fund, as well as the assets and liabilities of the Export Industries Fund. It would have an initial capitalisation of IKr 4 billion[74] with which to retire boats, reduce capacity in the processing industry and support investment in fishing and fish processing overseas by Icelandic firms[75]. The Fund would be supported in its early years by annual levies on fleet tonnage and on real estate owned by the fish-processing industry. The proposed fund is controversial – not so much because of these levies, but because it would, as of the autumn of 1996, introduce a new tax of one kronur per kilogram of cod-equivalent quota, indexed for increases in prices. Such a fee would be tiny[76], generating only about IKr 500 million per year in revenues. But vessel owners fear it would be a first step toward a full-scale "resource utilisation tax", removing much of the benefit accruing to owners of catch quota rights.

In principle, the current system, where the government assigns catch quotas and allows quota trading, could eventually lead to optimisation of the stream of net revenues accruing to Iceland from its fisheries – after a difficult transition period involving retirement of older workers and inefficient small boats. However, as it stands, the system could still be improved. In the long term net operating revenues per tonne are probably higher under the quota system than if no quota restrictions existed, more clearly so after excess small boats are retired. The government implicitly provided a rent or wealth transfer to those to whom it assigned the original quota rights, though some current owners paid a price for that rent by buying quota rights[77]. The implicit wealth transfer to quota owners may have been questionable from an overall social point of view, and the fisheries might therefore be expected to contribute more in taxes in return – once profits in the fisheries recover to more normal levels.

Independent of equity considerations, it is worth noting that a resource utilisation tax would, in any case, constitute a more efficient, less distortionary source of public funds than alternatives such as the income or even the value-added tax. With a moderate resource utilisation or quota tax[78], total fisheries output would be unaffected, still restrained by quota levels. In the long run, it would still pay producers to use least-cost production methods (such as large trawlers) – no distortions would be introduced in terms of resource utilisation. But the government would have the opportunity to reduce slightly the level of income or value-added taxation, and thereby reduce the economic distortions associated with the overall tax system.

IV.   Conclusions

1993 marked another year of economic stagnation for Iceland's economy. GDP growth of about 1 per cent in real terms was, however, better than expected: it was well above the OECD-Europe average and higher than in any year since 1987. But this performance is in part attributable to several factors which may not be fully sustained in coming years. The fish catch appears to have risen by about 4 per cent, defying predictions of a sharp fall, as the urgent adjustment to a serious decline in the stock of cod, Iceland's principal export product, was delayed into 1994, and the nation's fishermen again proved capable of dealing with adversity by diversifying into other, at least temporarily more plentiful species, by exploiting soon-to-be-closed loopholes in the quota system and by moving beyond local waters in search of more bountiful harvests. Processors also managed to maintain throughput by importing fish from foreign boats. But higher output did not translate into higher incomes due to a large decline in the terms of trade, led by a fall of nearly 14 per cent in world fish prices. Nevertheless, although at record levels, unemployment did not rise as much as had been feared, inflation proved fairly quiescent (especially considering the impact of the June devaluation on import costs), and the deficit on current account disappeared rather quickly.

However, it is unlikely that all of these favourable elements will continue to operate in 1994. The total allowable catch of cod has been cut by 20 per cent in the current fisheries year, and a disproportionate share of the catch had already been made by the end of 1993. With little prospect for a quota increase in the next fisheries year, the cod catch will almost certainly decline sharply. Even buttressed by modest gains in other exports, the external sector will cease providing support for growth, and the current account could remain in a nearly balanced position unless world fish prices recover strongly. Household demand will be constrained by a lack of income growth: employment could contract, wage rates are frozen, and personal taxes will provide little more than a modest stabilising influence. Government spending on goods and services is also budgeted to decline. Business investment is projected to remain weak, on account of the state of demand, although some support is expected from the reduction in interest rates. Overall, GDP may fall by 1 per cent in volume terms. Inevitably in such an environment, the unemployment rate will probably continue to rise to about 6 per cent, but consumer-price inflation could be more restrained than official projections (2 per cent) and could be effectively zero by year-end.

The prolonged economic stagnation is the price that Icelanders have to pay for the rebuilding of the cod stock following a combination of overfishing and unfavourable environmental conditions. No longer can the need to cut back on the annual cod catch be put off without seriously compromising its long-term future and even risking its eventual collapse. While there seems little risk from marine pollution from domestic sources, fisheries management remains the key structural policy challenge. In order for the system to succeed in maximising long-run net revenues from this renewable resource the overall allowable catch must be set no higher than the level considered safe by the nation's official marine biologists. The tradeable-quota system is an elegant and equitable means to achieve an efficient allocation of output, but its efficacy has been constrained by some loopholes which should be closed without further delay. In particular, the small-boat exemption – due to expire in September – is in part responsible for a clear excess of both capital and labour in the sector and for landings surpassing recommended catch levels. While the optimal pace at which small-boat capacity is retired is justifiably related to cyclical considerations, rationalisation must be pursued, despite the regional impacts (which could be offset, if necessary, by more direct and transparent measures). If profitability in the sector could be boosted and balance sheets improved, periodic pressures for devaluation by those involved in fishing would have less appeal. The proposal for a Fisheries Development Fund (to reduce capacity and support overseas fisheries activities) therefore deserves support, especially if it is financed by a quota tax. Such a tax can be justified by pointing to the significant resource rent component of fish prices and its distortion-free nature as a source of public revenues.

Another resource sector in serious need of further reform is agriculture. Despite important progress achieved as a result of the 1991 agreement between the government and the Farmers' Union, Iceland's farmers have benefited from one of the most heavily supported pricing and production systems in the OECD, achieved through a complex system of intervention and regulatory control. Insurmountable import barriers have indeed yielded a substantial degree of self-sufficiency, but at the cost of one of the highest relative prices of food of any Member country and a distorted cost structure, thereby inhibiting non-fisheries activities which could help reduce economic volatility. Cost-based producer price-setting by committee and controls on distribution margins have led to diminished incentives to utilise best-practice technology in order to achieve static and dynamic efficiency; this system should be deregulated as soon as possible in order to allow the market to determine appropriate prices. The significant budgetary component to the support system has imposed a heavy fiscal burden whose financing entails other macroeconomic pressures and costs and has helped push up public debt. The replacement of price and export subsidies by direct payments in 1992 and the concomitant 36 per cent decline in budgetary outlays on agriculture were laudable attempts to adjust production to declining domestic demand; these payments should now be totally decoupled from production and then gradually phased out in order to encourage further rationalisation of the sector. Other interventions in the form of levies to provide investment subsidies, protect domestic alternatives and cross-subsidise up- and downstream production should also be re-examined with a view to enhancing transparency and efficiency or possible elimination.

Indeed, Iceland's single most important environmental problem, soil erosion, has been indirectly exacerbated by the effects of agricultural policies. Overgrazing of livestock, production of which has been artificially stimulated by the support system, has aggravated an already serious long-term loss of vegetative cover due to harsh climatic conditions, especially in the more fragile highland region. To shift grazing toward the lowlands, the authorities have long pursued a policy of "land improvement", in part by fencing off the most sensitive areas. That, along with a drastic decline in the number of sheep over the last decade, has relieved grazing pressures, leaving only isolated cases of overgrazing. But reduction of price support would go a long way to alleviating the remaining problem.

Apart from soil erosion, Iceland's environment is in fine shape. Air quality is good and likely to get better, largely because of Iceland's location and minimal reliance on fossil fuels due to the abundance of hydroelectric and geothermal power. Recycling and proper treatment of solid and hazardous waste is rather limited at present, but the government has plans to improve such treatment substantially over the short and medium terms. Effluent treatment is rare, however, and while it may seem difficult to justify spending large sums to correct this, given the assimilative capacity of the oceans, over the longer term this would not only avoid localised water pollution problems, it would also serve to identify Iceland more clearly as "the cleanest country in the Western world". Capitalising on this image through expanding the tourism sector may require greater efforts to set aside land for nature conservation and protection. But even with strenuous adherence to the by now well-accepted "polluter/user pays principle", making further improvements to the environment is likely to prove costly and to boost the share of public spending devoted to this goal. It is therefore especially important that other lower-priority outlays be trimmed in order to avoid further budgetary problems.

Although the size of both the budget deficit and public indebtedness are less serious than in many other OECD countries, public debt has been rising steadily since the period of economic stagnation began in 1987. In recent years fiscal slippage has become a recurrent problem. An ambitious budget deficit target is usually set, but then changes during the course of the year to satisfy one group or another (often in the form of fiscal concessions to close the national wage negotiations) have meant that it has been missed, sometimes by a rather substantial amount. The result is a steady sizeable rise in public-sector indebtedness on both gross and net bases, although Treasury net debt is still only about 30 per cent of GDP. For 1994, the government has, however, probably been more realistic in its deficit objectives. It has taken some of the difficult decisions on where to cut spending in order to hold the line on overall outlays. Agricultural subsidies were an obvious target, paring back public investment expenditure may have been unavoidable, and reducing the government wage bill may have been only the first step in trying to boost public-sector efficiency. Looking beyond 1994, it is clear that braking the upward spiral of Treasury debt in relation to GDP will be possible only with further consolidation on the spending side, unless real GDP growth picks up substantially or there is a major improvement in the terms of trade. In any case, in order to enhance credibility, consideration should be given to the development of medium-term deficit-reduction targets.

The authorities have succeeded in maintaining a low-inflation environment. With unemployment about 6 per cent, wages are frozen for the remainder of the year, and the only source of inflationary pressure has been import costs. The June 1993 devaluation, the second in seven months, was understandable, given the implications of the reduction in the fish catch for the equilibrium value of the real exchange rate. Following the devaluation, the krona has been at its lowest level in real terms in some three decades, and overall cost competitiveness – aided by the reduction in corporate taxation – has been given a significant boost. But the devaluation has helped push foreign debt levels to new highs in kronur terms, even though they have been stable in foreign-currency terms; and the authorities face a difficulty in balancing the needs of the export sector and of the import-competing sector. The latter has been enjoying strong profits, but price weakness in the former has left its finances languishing. However, this financial pressure on exporters is to a large extent the result of the global economic slowdown and should recede in coming years, leaving them too with better profitability.

An additional success has been the move to lower interest rates. For some time the persistence of high interest rates, especially on indexed instruments, in the face of low inflation (both realised and expected) and meagre business demand for capital was a bit of a conundrum. The size of the public-sector borrowing requirement and the uncertainty surrounding its probable evolution, along with the persistent strength of household credit demands, were the best explanations available, but they seemed somewhat inadequate, and psychological barriers were probably important too. Indeed, as soon as the authorities acted aggressively to ease monetary policy in the autumn, the cost of borrowing fell across the board without any exchange-rate pressures. Also, the perverse fluctuations in bank intermediation margins would seem to have been efficiently dealt with for the time being by the series of swap contracts between the Central Bank and the deposit money banks, the former accepting some of the risk of short-term inflation fluctuations. But it seems that the longer-term solution is to allow the decline of indexation in the banking system, a relic from the former high-inflation era.

Increased competition in the financial sector and a broadening and deepening of domestic financial markets would also enforce reduced margins throughout the business cycle. Structural reforms in the financial system should help in this respect. The process of liberalising capital movements is now well advanced – Iceland has given up its derogation under the OECD Capital Movements Code – with important long-term benefits in view; securities-markets regulations have been modernised; a market for foreign exchange has been established; and the array of securities in the Treasury debt-management arsenal has been expanded. But the all-important revisions to the Central Bank Act, which would enhance its independence and clarify its objectives, remain in abeyance, as do plans to privatise one of the major banks.

Despite a rather disappointing year in terms of national income, and prospects for several more years of continued stagnation, very early indicators are that the replenishment of the cod stocks is on the medium-term horizon, thanks to the willingness of the authorities to manage the fisheries more prudently and to more favourable marine environmental conditions. With the entry into force of the European Economic Area agreement now accomplished, and given Iceland's advantages in a diversified range of natural and human resources, achievement of better outcomes later in the decade depends on the resolution of the remaining problems – notably the rise in public-sector and foreign indebtedness, still-high interest rates and a lack of competition in domestic markets. With continued attention paid to these questions, and vigilance to any revival of old difficulties such as inflation, the stage will be set for Iceland's return to a higher growth path.

Notes

1. The fisheries year begins 1 September. Estimates of fishable stocks and size of each year-class of cod are made each spring by the Marine Research Institute.

2. Official statistics – which may not fully reflect production by freezer trawlers nor the catch outside the 200 mile limit – show an increase of 3.6 per cent.

3. In all vessel groups there were boats which avoided losses and others which incurred large losses, but freezer trawlers were the only category which enjoyed positive profits as a whole.

4. This had little effect on the cod catch, where about 40 per cent the quota for the fisheries year had already been caught by year-end 1993. The strike ended when the government agreed to appoint a committee of officials to look into the matter. Their recommendation was for the establishment of an exchange through which all quota trading would pass in order to enhance transparency.

5. World demand fell about 1 per cent in 1993, the first decline since 1982. Exports from the FSU, mainly from Russia, rose from 300 000 tonnes in 1990 to 1.6 million tonnes in 1993. Correspondingly, London Metal Exchange prices were in the range of $0.47 per pound of aluminium late in 1993, down from $1.10 in early 1989. In January 1994 prices began to recover smartly, as Russian and western producers agreed to a substantial reduction in production and exports.

6. Net interest payments represented about 6.6 per cent of the net external debt in 1993, down from 7.2 per cent in 1992 and a peak of 9.1 per cent in 1989.

7. Semiannual labour market surveys, undertaken only since the early 1990s, suggest that the registered unemployment rate is usually somewhat lower than the rate based on the standardised ILO definition, but the difference was rarely more than a percentage point. By either definition, Iceland's unemployment rate is even now well below the OECD average.

8. The labour force participation rate peaked at about 79 per cent in 1989, coming down a bit in the recent fisheries downturn. Employment growth averaged 1.8 per cent in the 1980s.

9. This is not entirely to the good: it may hinder diversification and productivity growth by discouraging labour from flowing toward sectors where it might be more productive.

10. In past periods of strong income growth, "wage drift" upward has occurred, when secondary wage negotiations at the firm level allowed real wages in some sectors to rise faster than the nationally negotiated rate. Such secondary negotiations suggest scope for easing the transition for sectors where demand for labour is currently falling most severely. Local unions in the

hardest-hit sectors could be encouraged to negotiate for less severe job cuts in exchange for additional wage concessions beyond the nationally agreed contract.

11. This apparent contradiction is explained in part by the effects of the November devaluation on dollar-denominated government debt, as well as the financing of the Treasury overdraft at the Central Bank stemming from the large deficit in 1991.

12. The local turnover tax, which was a major source of revenue for the municipalities (Reykjavik in particular), amounted to an average of 1 per cent of business turnover. Prior to 1993, the statutory corporate income tax rate had been 45 per cent, well above the European average (which was roughly 39 per cent in 1990). Iceland's corporate tax rate was reduced to 39 per cent in 1993, and to 33 per cent in 1994, from a recent peak of 50 per cent in 1988.

13. These tax increases included a 1.5 percentage point rise in the personal income tax rate, a temporary 5 per cent surcharge on high-income households and a cut in the personal exemption. However, these tax increases (plus transfer to municipalities) by the central government were explicitly temporary. In 1994, the Treasury ended the arrangement: municipalities now raise those revenues directly, having increased their local personal income tax rates by an average of 1.6 percentage points. This will boost local tax receipts by about Ikr 2.9 billion – the remainder of their revenue shortfall from the abolition of the turnover tax is being made up by increasing property taxes on business. The Treasury has made room for this last by abolishing its own property tax on office and commercial buildings.

14. The unions later argued that the actual addition to public investment spending for 1993 was less than the rise negotiated in May. In November, after further discussions, the government agreed to add a further IKr 335 million in spending on road construction – in 1994. This addition to government construction spending was financed by a tax increase on gasoline and diesel fuel effective January 1994.

15. Overall GDP growth was predicted fairly accurately in the budget document, but the composition differed in ways that had important implications for employment. Fisheries output was stronger than expected, but this had very few implications for employment in the sector – changes in fisheries output tend to affect productivity rather than labour usage. On the other hand, output outside of the fisheries was weaker than expected, and in this part of the economy lower output does result in reduced employment. Unanticipated changes in the mix of output probably contributed to the underestimate of the unemployment rate in the 1993 budget.

16. Even though GDP growth for 1993 was in line with the projected figure in the initial budget proposal of October 1992, real national income turned out about 1½ percentage points short of the level anticipated at that early stage. In particular, fish prices were not expected to fall as much as they have done. By December 1992, however, the government projection for real national income growth in 1993 was revised downward to a figure close to the actual outcome.

17. Total slippage due to the three factors was actually a bit greater, at about IKr 6 billion. However, that gross slippage was offset in part by an unexpected fall in gross interest payments of IKr 600 million and by additional revenues resulting from more effective tax collection and greater interest income.

18. However, the increase will be partially offset by a decline in the sector's social-security payroll tax from 6 to 2½ per cent.

19. This will be achieved by cutting the wage bill through attrition and reduction in overtime, while wage rates remain unchanged through the end of 1994, and by increased efficiency achieved in part by merging several institutions.

20. These figures include both central- and local-government debt. For the Treasury alone, gross debt at end-1994 is projected to be about 45 per cent of GDP and net debt about 30 per cent of GDP.

21. The formula for debt stabilisation is $S = D^* (i - G)/(1 + G)$ where S is the ratio of the primary surplus to GDP, D is the beginning-of-year ratio of net debt to GDP, i is the average interest rate on the debt and G is the nominal growth rate of output. This is equivalent to $S = D^* (r - q)/(1 + p + q)$ where r is the real interest rate, q is the real growth rate and p is the inflation rate. For Iceland, D is .303 and p can be taken to be near zero.

22. Previously, the Central Bank set the bid and asked exchange rates unilaterally on a daily basis, and the deposit-money banks transacted with their clients at those rates throughout the day. They were required to balance their foreign-currency-denominated assets and liabilities. Under the new system, a fixing meeting of market participants is held each morning, but the banks are free to deal at other rates at other times and may take net foreign currency positions of up to 10 per cent of equity capital for each currency and 20 per cent in total. In the event their position has varied between 12 and 16 per cent of such capital. Total transaction volumes have averaged about 1 per cent of GDP per month, with the Central Bank involved in well over half of all transactions.

23. Since the official fluctuation limits are defined in terms of the krona price of the foreign-currency basket, these bands were increased by an average of 8.1 per cent.

24. These figures are on a trade-weighted basis; for the official currency basket adopted at end-1991 (with weights of 76 per cent on the ECU, 18 per cent on the dollar and 6 per cent on the yen), the cumulative devaluation has been about 2 percentage points greater.

25. It should be noted that such yields were in excess of 8 per cent through much of 1991.

26. It also cut the repo rate three more times by year-end, bringing that rate down a further 1½ points.

27. The minimum maturity of indexed loans was cut from 3 to 2 years, while that on deposits was raised from 6 to 12 months. Also, from end-1994 the imbalance between the DMBs' indexed assets and liabilities must be no more than 20 per cent of own capital.

28. In May the Treasury borrowed £100 million in the form of ten-year bonds at 8.75 per cent. In July it issued $125 million of five-year bonds at 6 per cent.

29. No foreign entry is allowed in the fishing, primary fish processing, energy production and energy distribution sectors, and foreign participation in the banking and aviation sectors is limited to 25 and 49 per cent, respectively. Under the European Economic Area agreement all restrictions except the ban on investment in fishing and fish processing will be modified by end-1995.

30. The State's guarantee is worth some 25 basis points in terms of lower interest rates.

31. One exception has been a small fund established in the early 1990s to promote employment of women in rural areas, where job opportunities are generally more limited and unemployment higher for women than men. The programme involves spending of IKr 15 million per year (*versus* GDP of about IKr 385 billion) on job training and consultancy relative to job creation.

32. Plants grow for only four months – from May to September.

33. The recently implemented European Economic Area agreement also involved the elimination of import duties on some fruit and vegetables originating within the area.

34. The government-guaranteed debt of fur farmers was written off in 1993.

35. Indirect competition is provided by imported processed food products and ready-made food.

36. A major review of Icelandic agriculture by the Directorate for Food, Agriculture and Fisheries has just got underway.

37. The basic law on production, pricing and sale of agricultural products of 1985 includes the following among its objectives: ''to ensure that the production of agricultural products will be at a level that will satisfy the national needs ... to ensure that domestic factors of production will be utilised to the extent possible for agricultural production, with respect both to security of production and employment...''

38. Because of its isolation, Iceland's livestock has not acquired any resistance to certain animal diseases, common in other countries. Accordingly, the nation has suffered several incidents of the introduction of infectious diseases through the import of live animals and raw food. The most famous example was the destruction of 40 per cent of the sheep stock due to Maedi and Jones disease from imports of Karakul sheep from Germany in the late 1920s.

39. Unfortunately, the only data available to this point for the ''consumer subsidy equivalent'' (CSE) in Iceland are from unofficial sources (Johannsson and Olafsson, 1993). This work points to a CSE of about 3 per cent of private consumption (2 per cent of GDP), second highest among the five Nordic countries (after Finland), a group that is highly protected by international standards. It also argues that agricultural trade restrictions alone cost Icelandic consumers some 2.4 per cent of total private consumption, nearly 14 per cent of food consumption. Lipsey and Swedenborg (1993) have shown that the main explanation for persistently high food prices in a sample of OECD countries is the extent of protection of agricultural products at the farm level.

40. For a more lengthy discussion of the problem of the concentration of economic activity, and especially of exports, on the fisheries and the resulting increase in economic volatility, see the previous OECD Survey of Iceland.

41. The government also makes payments to the Agricultural Productivity Fund in order to support alternative employment for farmers and strengthen the sector. Such payments have fallen from IKr 666 million in 1991 to 250 million in 1994.

42. Nevertheless, budgetary outlays are usually a more desirable form of support, given their transparency and tractability, than other, less direct measures.

43. Until a few years ago, producer prices of potatoes were also administered. It should also be noted that the poultry and egg sectors were exposed for the first time to a quota system as recently as 1988, but without any government guarantees: the only discipline is that above-

quota production does not benefit from reimbursement of feed levies nor a portion of VAT (until 1994, when VAT refunding is being eliminated simultaneous with the new lower rate on food – see Chapter II). Despite the quota system, price wars are frequent, given the oligopolistic structure of the market.

44.   Surplus milk production reached a peak of over 20 000 tonnes (17½ per cent of total production) in 1985 but has most recently fallen to 0.5 per cent of production. For sheepmeat a similar story unfolds: surplus production has fallen from over 3 000 tonnes (nearly a quarter of production) in 1985 to some 800 tonnes (still 9 per cent of production).

45.   International price comparisons are sensitive to quality differences and therefore must be treated with caution. Official Nordic data show that in 1988 wholesale prices were higher than anywhere else in the region for milk, eggs and potatoes and second highest for most of the other items examined (flour, butter, beef, bacon). Complete producer-price data for all OECD countries, when available, are given in Annex I, Tables 1 to 6.

46.   The level of the quota (''support target'') is renegotiated every year. Domestic per capita dairy-product consumption in milk-equivalent terms has fallen from 456 litres in 1976 to 380 litres in 1992. Similarly, sheepmeat consumption per capita fell from 49 kg. in 1975 to 30 kg. in 1992. However, the quota for 1991-92 was still about 50 per cent greater than demand. It has only been in 1993-94 that quota has been cut sufficiently (by a cumulative 38 per cent) to meet estimated domestic consumption.

47.   Based on the draft budget for 1994, direct Treasury spending on agriculture would be 40 per cent lower than average outlays in the previous parliamentary term.

48.   The authorities now recognise that this system has worked against rationalisation in the dairy industry; accordingly, the price equalisation fund is to be abolished within the next few years. Until recently, a similar system was in operation for the slaughtering of sheep.

49.   In that period, the proceeds of the levy were used to subsidise sheepmeat and dairy exports and the state-owned fertiliser plant – which has a monopoly on the production and sale of fertiliser until the end of 1994. It is required to sell at a single price at all harbours, thereby providing free transport to remote areas.

50.   For a detailed description of the PSE/CSE methodology see, for example, OECD (1993*d*, Annex III).

51.   According to earlier estimates made by researchers at the University of Iceland (Johansson and Olaffson, 1993), using a concept different from that used by the OECD, total support in 1988 amounted to over IKr 10 billion (4.1 per cent of GDP and 110.7 per cent of farm production value); 42 per cent of the total came in the form of market support; a further 30 per cent in direct domestic price support (subsidies); another 8 per cent for export subsidies; and the remainder in indirect support and miscellaneous services. Support was uniformly high but variable across products. Most of the difference seems to come from the fact that the University figures do not take the same measurement approach as do the government figures, which are intended to conform to the PSE concept. There are also some notable differences in the values of production used for sheepmeat and, especially, beef. Finally, there appears to have been double counting in some of the calculations of support levels.

52. This is in sharp contrast with the rest of the OECD, where PSEs are lowest for poultry (12 per cent in 1992, compared to 44 per cent over all products) and eggs (7 per cent).

53. There has been, however, a recent reversal in the trend decline in the application of artificial fertilisers: from 30 700 tonnes in 1979, consumption fell to 21 700 tonnes in 1988 before recovering to 22 700 tonnes in 1991. Iceland uses about one third more nitrogenous fertiliser per hectare than the OECD average, but still only about one sixth as much as in the Netherlands. Total pesticide use also declined from the early to mid-1980s, but by 1991 had regained its early-1980s level. Note that internationally there seems to be a significant positive exponential relationship between the intensity of both fertiliser and pesticide use and the percentage PSE (Parris and Melanie, 1993).

54. The share of the nation's surface area which is made up of barren land has increased substantially over the centuries. Information regarding more recent trends is spotty, but the process has clearly slowed in recent decades, although it has probably not been totally arrested: soil lost through erosion still appears to exceed that regained through reclamation and natural revegetation.

55. The total plant biomass production capacity of the rangelands is estimated to be as little as one fifth of its pre-settlement capacity.

56. It should be borne in mind that grazing problems related to horses are mostly limited to confined areas in the lowlands.

57. In practice, most of the land is either owned or governed by farmers, and therefore grazing fees would not be applicable in such cases.

58. The national government has for several years been promoting the consolidation of municipal governments, but not for environmental reasons.

59. Output of food fish jumped from 50 tonnes in 1983 to over 1 500 tonnes in 1989.

60. While it appears from the table that spending declined in 1993, actual outlays may well have exceeded budgeted levels: for example, overspending in 1991 and 1992 amounted to some 27 and 15 per cent, respectively.

61. Including fish processing, the sector is responsible for about 16 per cent of GDP, about 11 per cent of employment, 80 per cent of merchandise exports and 57 per cent of total exports.

62. These traces are to a large extent attributable to long-range transport of these persistent chemicals from Europe and North America.

63. Some cesium is reported in Icelandic waters, possibly from the Sellafield plant. Atmospheric transport of persistent organohalogens is also a concern.

64. Stocks of most other species, with the possible exception of redfish, are in satisfactory condition. In general, fish stocks are also a function of several exogenous and yet probably interdependent factors, mostly rather imperfectly understood: *i)* the level of recruitment, that is the entry of young fish into the fishing grounds; *ii)* the growth rate of individual fish – for example, feeding conditions for cod deteriorated from 1988 to 1990 in part because of an inflow of cold Arctic water, which resulted in a fall of some 10 per cent in the average weight of a six-year-old cod in 1990; *iii)* the age of sexual maturity; and *iv)* migratory flows.

65. The average spawning stock estimate over the past decade is only 18 per cent of the original 1955 estimate.

66. Equally important, quota loopholes remain open in the 1993/94 fisheries year, and this may add another 15 or 20 per cent to the excess over MRI recommendations – though the government's proposed revisions to the general law on the fisheries might close those loopholes before the peak summer season for small boat activity. These proposed changes to the fisheries law would allow fish processing firms to own quota rights, and would convert small boats to catch quotas over the course of the 1993/94 season.

67. Under this effort-quota system, more restrictions were placed on cod fishing than on fishing for other species. Beginning in 1991, virtually all boats were subject to catch quotas, though some of the catch of boats using ''longlines'' instead of nets to fish was exempt. However, for a transition period lasting until 1 September 1994, smaller boats are subject to effort rather than catch quotas.

68. The small-boat exemption to the catch-quota system (until September 1994) has most recently allowed effort-quota landings of about 22 000 tonnes per year of cod (9.3 per cent of the total catch) and smaller amounts of other groundfish. In addition to the small-boat ''loophole'', the quota system has four other exemptions. First, half the longline catch made in the four winter months – about 5 per cent of the total catch for cod and about the same for haddock – is not counted in the attributed quota. (In setting quotas, the Ministry of Fisheries has overestimated the winter longline catch in recent years; however, starting in 1994/95 longliners will instead be assigned fixed overall catch quotas for the entire fisheries year). Second, undersized (young) fish are also partially exempt – they represent some 2 per cent of the cod catch, 1½ per cent for haddock and 0.7 per cent for redfish. Third, other than for cod, quotas can be exceeded by up to 5 per cent, with offsetting compensation on the vessel's quota of other demersal species. Finally, vessel owners can carry unused quota either forward (as much as 20 per cent for some species) or backward (as much as 5 per cent), but the impact of this provision is, of course, zero over time.

69. Note that the proceeds from quota sales upon exit from the industry accrue solely to the owner of the vessel.

70. There is a proposal to allow processing factories to buy quota up to an amount equal to the average of their throughput in the last three years.

71. Similar shares of the permanent catch quotas for other groundfish are traded.

72. Equity represents an average of only about one quarter of total capital. Thus, industry fluctuations generate immense volatility in financial performance and intense pressures for policy changes to damp them.

73. The Fund is financed through an annual fee imposed on all fishing vessels over 10 GRT, yielding IKr 80 million per year, and through a share (along with the MRI) of the proceeds from the sale of an annual catch quota of 12 000 tonnes per year, worth an estimated IKr 400 million.

74. This would be provided in the form of a loan from the government bearing market rates of interest and to be repaid within a decade. The Fund would therefore have no subsidy element.

75. Recent investments have been made in Germany and Chile, for example.

76.   This can be seen by a comparison with the market price of annual quota which in the last few years has averaged about IKr 40 per kilogram, about half of the landed price of the fish.

77.   It is for this reason that it would be entirely appropriate to announce such a tax well before its imposition.

78.   The current quota system can be thought of as equivalent to an annual tax on catch tonnage (to bring production in line with external costs), offset by an equal lump-sum transfer to holders of catch quotas. A quota tax would have the effect of reducing the compensating lump-sum transfer to quota holders.

References

Baldursson, Fridrik M., Asgeir Danielsson and Gunnar Stefansson (1993), "On the rational utilization of the Icelandic cod stock", Paper prepared for the ICES statutory meeting.

Gylfason, T. (1990), "Iceland in the Outskirts of Europe: The Common Property Resource Problem", Paper presented to the Conference on EFTA Countries in a Changing Europe, Geneva, November.

Johannsson, Kristjan and Sigurdur Olafsson (1993), *Landbrugspolitik og husholdningers okonomi*, Nordisk Ministerrad, Nord 1993:9, Copenhagen.

Lipsey, Robert E. and Birgitta Swedenborg (1993), "The High Cost of Eating: Agricultural Protection and International Differences in Consumer Food Prices", Working Paper No. 4555, National Bureau of Economic Research, Cambridge, Massachusetts, December.

Marine Research Institute (1993), *State of Marine Stocks in Icelandic Waters 1992/93; Prospects for the Quota Year 1993/94*, Reykjavik, 25 June.

Ministry for the Environment (1992), *Iceland: National Report to UNCED*, Reykjavik.

Ministry for the Environment (1993), *Towards Sustainable Development – National Environmental Strategy of Iceland*, Reykjavik.

OECD (1993a), *Agriculture and Environmental Policy Integration: Recent Progress and New Directions*, Paris.

OECD (1993b), *Iceland Environmental Performance Review*, Paris.

OECD (1993c), "Assessing the relative transfer efficiency of agricultural support policies", OECD Working Papers, Vol. II, No. 9.

OECD (1993d), *Agricultural Policies, Markets and Trade: Monitoring and Outlook 1993*, Paris.

OECD (1994), "Agricultural Policy Reform: Environmental Externalities and Public Goods" in *Agricultural Policy Reform: New Approaches*, Paris.

Parris, Kevin and Jane Melanie (1993), "Japan's agriculture and environmental policies: time to change", *Agriculture and Resources Quarterly*, 3, 5, September.

Winters, L. Alan (1987), "The Economic Consequences of Agricultural Support: A Survey", *OECD Economic Studies*, 9, Autumn.

Annex I

Supplementary material to Chapter III:
agriculture, resource management and the environment

Table A.1. **Producer prices for poultry in OECD countries**

	Nominal producer prices National currency/100 kg	Nominal producer prices $/100 kg	Index of real producer prices[1] (1984 = 100)				
	1993	1993	1988	1990	1991	1992	1993
Iceland	**30 000.0**	**444.6**	**84.7**	**81.3**	**76.6**	**70.9**	**78.2**
Canada	164.2	127.3	80.3	80.6	75.4	73.2	73.9
United States	79.1	79.1	66.3	60.5	55.2	55.3	54.9
Japan	25 930.0	233.6	66.1	69.1	70.8	67.9	63.2
Australia	170.9	116.1	93.4	85.8	77.6	74.9	76.1
New Zealand	185.3	100.2	72.4	72.3	69.6	66.2	64.6
EC-12	121.6	142.5	71.4	63.1	61.1	57.1	56.8
Austria	2 155.0	185.3	92.9	89.5	89.3	83.6	79.3
Finland	1 229.8	215.0	86.0	79.4	77.7	73.1	70.0
Norway	2 265.0	319.6	103.7	99.7	98.5	95.8	92.0
Sweden	1 213.9	156.2	88.5	79.6	69.7	66.5	66.7
Switzerland	505.0	341.8	91.1	88.5	79.0	74.3	72.4

1. Deflated by the GDP implicit price deflator.
Source: OECD, Directorate for Food, Agriculture and Fisheries, and Economics Department; National Economic Institute.

Table A.2. **Producer prices for eggs in OECD countries**

	Nominal producer prices National currency/100 kg	Nominal producer prices $/100 kg	Index of real producer prices [1] (1984 = 100)				
	1993	1993	1988	1990	1991	1992	1993
Iceland	**24 450**	**362.4**	**78.1**	**79.7**	**75.2**	**75.0**	**75.2**
Canada	161	124.9	88.0	81.1	80.3	83.1	83.8
United States	90	90.2	64.5	79.0	72.6	60.1	65.0
Japan	14 600	131.5	63.4	89.9	79.3	56.6	56.1
Australia	186	126.0	73.7	62.8	61.7	60.9	60.4
New Zealand	178	96.3	54.6	55.3	43.5	42.7	41.9
EC-12	109	127.2	64.8	64.7	61.3	55.3	58.0
Austria	1 875	161.2	78.7	78.9	75.8	70.4	66.8
Finland	887	155.1	73.5	65.0	62.6	62.2	60.1
Norway	1 375	194.0	101.7	89.4	91.9	88.8	82.7
Sweden	769	99.0	79.3	71.9	63.8	57.5	57.7
Switzerland	630	426.5	101.0	96.6	93.6	94.1	86.6

1. Deflated by the GDP implicit price deflator.
Source: OECD, Directorate for Food, Agriculture and Fisheries, and Economics Department; National Economic Institute.

Table A.3. **Producer prices for beef in OECD countries**

	Nominal producer prices National currency/100 kg	Nominal producer prices $/100 kg	Index of real producer prices [1] (1984 = 100)				
	1993 Carcass-weight basis		1988	1990	1991	1992	1993
Iceland	**26 270**	**390.0**	**91.1**	**93.1**	**94.1**	**79.2**	**76.5**
Canada	352	272.6	90.8	83.2	78.7	79.7	91.2
United States	283	283.0	107.5	113.8	109.1	101.0	101.5
Japan	12 880	1 160.3	102.8	103.3	94.6	87.5	83.2
Australia	226	153.5	94.4	86.1	81.0	79.4	92.4
New Zealand	270	146.1	59.8	62.2	62.7	64.6	64.4
EC-12	337	394.2	91.7	80.5	72.5	69.8	74.1
Austria	4 552	391.4	84.8	85.0	79.4	73.3	70.3
Finland	2 348	410.5	93.1	88.9	78.2	76.8	71.2
Norway	3 233	456.2	100.3	93.2	91.3	90.5	86.3
Sweden	2 563	329.7	110.8	82.1	81.5	79.1	75.3
Switzerland	920	622.8	98.1	80.8	66.1	58.8	62.9
			Index of real producer prices [1] (1986 = 100)				
Memorandum items:							
EC [2]	337	394.2	93.1	81.7	73.5	70.7	75.2
Belgium	11 399	330.2	94.6	85.1	74.1	77.0	76.1
Denmark	1 875	289.6	92.2	84.0	73.4	70.8	68.6
France	2 090	369.4	99.9	94.9	83.6	83.6	84.9
Germany	537	352.2	95.7	89.2	74.5	74.2	72.1
Greece	86 760	379.3	93.4	91.3	82.2	90.9	90.9
Ireland	202	296.4	113.3	97.7	91.9	92.1	97.6
Italy	5 543	347.3	89.1	80.5	73.3	72.3	82.2
Netherlands	592	319.0	101.6	91.1	80.3	84.8	85.0
Spain	45 570	359.7	104.2	82.1	74.7	66.1	75.9
United Kingdom	217	326.1	103.1	81.9	76.7	76.0	86.8

1. Deflated by the GDP implicit price deflator.
2. EC individual country data have been converted from ECUs and transferred to a carcass-weight basis by dividing the live-weight source data by 0.55.

Source: OECD, Directorate for Food, Agriculture and Fisheries, and Economics Department; National Economic Institute.

Table A.4. **Producer prices for pigmeat in OECD countries**

	Nominal producer prices National currency/100 kg	Nominal producer prices $/100 kg	Index of real producer prices [1] (1984 = 100)				
	1993 Carcass-weight basis	1993	1988	1990	1991	1992	1993
Iceland	**37 000.0**	**548.0**	**87.4**	**86.6**	**84.7**	**85.0**	**86.3**
Canada	164.0	127.2	75.1	83.2	72.5	66.1	76.9
United States	138.1	138.1	78.4	91.4	82.3	66.9	70.5
Japan	41 000.0	369.3	64.9	60.7	63.5	64.7	58.6
Australia	201.3	136.7	91.4	88.2	76.4	74.8	83.4
New Zealand	251.5	136.0	63.7	72.1	63.8	65.0	61.5
EC-12	126.3	147.9	65.1	66.9	63.7	64.1	49.9
Austria	2 447.7	210.5	78.8	79.8	80.0	77.1	67.9
Finland	1 570.9	274.6	90.3	84.2	77.5	75.6	73.9
Norway	2 578.0	363.8	103.7	99.0	97.1	91.7	84.1
Sweden	1 399.4	180.1	90.9	77.9	76.9	70.2	66.5
Switzerland	519.9	351.9	82.5	82.3	78.4	63.7	63.0
			Index of real producer prices [1] (1987 = 100)				
Memorandum items:							
EC [2]	126	147.9	93.6	96.1	91.6	92.1	71.9
Belgium	5 511	159.6	94.4	104.8	102.6	101.8	75.0
Denmark	837	129.2	95.7	86.6	83.0	86.2	65.3
France	790	139.7	92.8	102.0	99.2	98.6	68.2
Germany	248	150.1	93.3	106.0	104.7	102.4	73.9
Greece	42 130	184.2	96.5	104.7	93.4	101.3	83.1
Ireland	103	150.5	99.5	107.1	101.3	107.3	92.7
Italy	280 480	178.6	97.9	96.7	94.1	98.7	84.5
Netherlands	246	132.3	90.8	99.2	98.9	95.9	68.6
Spain	19 440	153.4	89.0	86.1	81.6	80.9	67.6
United Kingdom	103	155.3	87.8	91.6	78.3	84.5	76.0

1. Deflated by the GDP implicit price deflator.
2. EC individual country data have been converted from ECUs.
Source: OECD, Directorate for Food, Agriculture and Fisheries, and Economics Department; National Economic Institute.

91

Table A.5. **Producer prices for sheepmeat in OECD countries**

	Nominal producer prices National currency/100 kg	Nominal producer prices $/100 kg	Index of real producer prices [1] (1984 = 100)				
	1993	1993	1988	1990	1991	1992	1993
Iceland [2]	**42 710**	**633.0**	**102.6**	**95.7**	**96.7**	**93.6**	**92.3**
Canada	604	468.0	101.8	83.8	95.7	110.0	134.1
United States	238	238.1	115.5	84.0	77.5	79.5	83.2
Japan	n.a.	n.a.	n.a.	n.a.	n.a.	n.a.	n.a.
Australia	67	45.8	92.3	31.6	41.2	59.6	55.7
New Zealand	209	112.7	69.4	97.6	85.3	121.9	124.1
EC-12	312	365.4	83.0	66.3	56.7	56.5	53.1
Austria	5 227	449.6	87.1	86.5	84.8	83.2	80.0
Finland	2 197	384.1	105.2	105.9	95.6	87.2	79.0
Norway	2 568	362.3	99.9	79.4	79.4	83.1	76.6
Sweden	1 975	254.2	101.3	80.1	65.7	69.6	65.3
Switzerland	1 300	880.0	102.5	103.0	93.5	81.7	82.4

n.a. = not available.
1. Deflated by the GDP implicit price deflator.
2. Including direct payments.
Source: OECD, Directorate for Food, Agriculture and Fisheries, and Economics Department; National Economic Institute.

Table A.6. **Producer prices for milk in OECD countries**

	Nominal producer prices National currency/100 kg	Nominal producer prices $/100 kg	Index of real producer prices [1] (1984 = 100)				
	1993	1993	1988	1990	1991	1992	1993
Iceland [2]	510.0	75.7	94.5	95.8	92.6	95.1	91.1
Canada [3]	44.2	34.3	94.8	90.5	90.4	93.2	91.4
United States	28.3	28.2	79.6	81.6	70.2	73.0	69.5
Japan	8 947.5	80.6	87.6	85.8	84.2	82.4	82.0
Australia [3]	30.3	20.6	111.3	98.7	105.9	114.6	110.6
New Zealand	29.6	16.0	84.4	61.4	76.6	84.1	83.2
EC-12	29.3	34.3	88.4	82.6	76.3	73.5	72.7
Austria	490.2	42.2	91.8	90.3	89.1	87.1	85.0
Finland	286.6	50.1	92.1	88.9	88.5	85.9	86.2
Norway	284.2	40.1	144.0	165.9	162.7	179.9	167.8
Sweden	296.9	38.2	99.2	74.5	71.4	69.6	67.6
Switzerland	86.0	58.2	95.1	87.5	84.4	82.1	78.3
			Index of real producer prices [1] (1986 = 100)				
Memorandum items:							
EC [4]	29	34.3	97.0	90.8	83.8	80.6	80.0
Belgium	1 245	36.1	103.6	96.1	84.9	89.3	92.4
Denmark	256	39.6	99.5	100.7	90.9	88.0	84.7
France	191	33.8	97.6	97.7	92.8	92.4	91.0
Germany	61	36.9	99.8	92.9	87.8	84.3	78.4
Greece	8 015	35.0	92.5	93.4	85.9	89.0	84.6
Ireland	20	29.7	109.7	105.0	99.6	107.9	108.2
Italy	61 373	39.1	92.6	91.1	84.1	81.1	79.9
Netherlands	68	36.4	108.5	88.8	88.6	87.5	85.2
Spain	3 778	29.8	92.5	79.9	70.9	66.6	68.8
United Kingdom	19	28.5	95.7	92.2	93.9	94.6	85.6

1. Deflated by the GDP implicit price deflator.
2. Including direct payments.
3. Data for Australia and Canada have been converted to a kilogram basis by multiplying the litres of the source data by 1.03.
4. EC individual country data has been converted from ECUs.
Source: OECD, Directorate for Food, Agriculture and Fisheries, and Economics Department; National Economic Institute.

Main economic events

1993

January

EEA membership approved by the Althing. Regulations regarding short-term capital movements liberalised in line with the EEA agreement: capital movements and foreign exchange transactions related to imports and exports of goods and services are now unconstrained, though the Central Bank can temporarily limit short-term capital movements if they cause exchange-rate instability.

New regime for the reimbursement of drug purchases and for ambulatory and specialist care.

February

Central Bank and Treasury agree to end direct access of Treasury to borrowing from Central Bank, except for the first 3-5 days of the month under extraordinary circumstances.

March

Althing passes new legislation on securities transactions, mutual funds and the stock exchange – changes take effect 1 July 1993.

Central Bank lowers the discount rate to Icelandic banks by 1 to 3 percentage points. At the same time, the Central Bank cuts by 1.5 percentage points the repurchase rates on Treasury bills and notes, driving down market yields correspondingly.

May

The Althing passes new legislation on deposit money banks.

National wage agreement is passed, freezing wage rates (tentatively through end-1994, with the freeze to be reviewed in November 1993). Government promises a further reduction in interest rates, a shift toward foreign rather than domestic borrowing, and a reduction in the VAT on food in January 1994. It also promises, among other things, increased expenditures on public works projects, lower excise duties on construction materials, and spending to cushion losses of lowest-income groups.

Treasury issues one-year notes for the first time.

A new foreign exchange market is established.

June

Repurchase rate cut in two stages by a further percentage point.

On 28 June the government devalues the krona 7.5 per cent, in response to falling fish prices and a 40 000 ton reduction in the cod quota for 1993/94.

The sale of Treasury bills on tap ceases at months end.

July

Rules changed regarding indexation on financial markets, to reduce excess volatility of unindexed bank loans: indexation of bank loans is allowed for maturities as short as two years, while indexation of time deposits of less than one year's maturity is now forbidden.

August

On-tap sales of Treasury notes cease.

September

Central Bank agrees to an interest rate swap with deposit money banks, to reduce their indexation-related exposure to inflation risk. Agreement is to be renewed every four months for the next 2½ years – but at that point, the government will stop assuming banks' inflation risk in this way.

October

The government publishes its draft national budget for 1994.

Repurchase rate cut by a further percentage point.

The government announces it will no longer accept bids for indexed government bonds at real rates in excess of 5 per cent – domestic yields on government bonds fall by about 2 percentage points.

World prices of fish turn up for the first time since early 1992.

November

Unions confirm the extension of the wage freeze through end-1994.

Repurchase rate cut in two stages by a further percentage point.

December

The 1994 budget is passed by the Althing. It cuts back on public works spending from 1993 and features a variety of tax changes, some already planned in the 1993 budget. Tax reductions include a drop in the corporate tax rate from 39 to 33 per cent and a reduction from 24.5 to 14 per cent in the VAT on food. Tax increases include a rise in personal tax rates by 0.35 percentage points, a new 10 per cent tax on capital income effective in late 1994, and a 30 per cent increase in taxes on automobile purchases. With weaker national income in 1994, the budget targets a small deterioration in the Treasury deficit.

Repurchase rate cut another ½ percentage point.

1994

January

The EEA agreement takes effect, increasing access of Icelandic goods, services and labour to EC markets. Most importantly, EC tariffs on Icelandic fish products are reduced.

VAT on food is reduced from 24.5 per cent to 14 per cent, while a VAT tax is introduced on hotel services. Corporate income tax rates fall to 33 per cent, while personal income tax increase of 0.35 percentage points is introduced.

A strike idles the fishing industry for two weeks. Unions felt that boat owners were violating union contracts by trading quotas over the counter in ways that deducted the price of purchased quotas from catch value before the proceeds from sale of the catch were divided up with crew members. To settle the strike, the government sets up a commission: it proposes to require quota trading to operate only through a formal trading exchange.

The unemployment rate soars to an unadjusted rate of 7.7 per cent.

United States and Iceland sign a new two-year treaty, reaffirming the 1951 agreement for U.S. defence of Iceland if attacked. However, the treaty also calls for reduction in the NATO presence at Keflavik air force base, including two thirds of the contingent of U.S. fighter aircraft.

February

The Icelandic State Herring Oil and Meal Factories are privatised through sale to a consortium of 21 fishing firms and 4 financial firms for $10.3 million.

Various trade disputes break out: with France over fish exports and with Canada over imports of French fries and chicken breasts.

STATISTICAL AND STRUCTURAL ANNEX

Table A. **Supply and use of resources**

IKr million, current prices

	1983	1984	1985	1986	1987	1988	1989	1990	1991	1992	1993
Private consumption	39 432	53 930	74 689	96 072	129 795	156 203	184 435	213 555	236 276	236 213	236 592
Public consumption	11 978	14 595	20 954	28 419	38 529	49 895	59 503	68 854	76 918	78 930	82 592
Gross fixed asset formation	14 127	18 356	24 460	29 684	41 042	48 414	56 051	66 896	72 700	66 447	61 300
Expenditure on final domestic use	65 537	86 881	120 103	154 175	209 366	254 512	299 989	349 305	385 894	381 590	380 484
Change in stocks of export products	-1 070	786	-978	-2 094	-416	1 850	-578	-1 787	1 233	123	2 174
National expenditure	64 467	87 667	119 125	152 081	208 950	256 362	299 411	347 518	387 127	381 713	382 658
Exports of goods and services	27 078	34 295	49 534	62 888	73 085	83 548	108 335	126 456	127 231	123 528	137 277
Imports of goods and services	25 275	33 871	48 663	55 880	73 965	84 100	99 240	119 595	130 305	121 943	122 581
Gross domestic product (market prices)	66 270	88 091	119 996	159 089	208 070	255 810	308 506	354 379	384 053	383 298	397 354
Net income from abroad	-3 066	-4 554	-5 584	-6 229	-6 203	-8 333	-13 217	-14 611	-14 974	-13 585	-14 358
Gross national product	63 204	83 537	114 412	152 860	201 867	247 477	295 289	339 768	369 079	369 713	382 996
Depreciation	8 780	10 697	14 552	18 542	22 086	27 346	35 218	41 382	45 994	49 296	50 500
Net national product (market prices)	54 424	72 840	99 860	134 318	179 781	220 131	260 071	298 386	323 085	320 417	332 496
Indirect taxes	14 486	20 062	26 341	33 964	46 314	58 875	69 133	75 544	80 135	79 881	82 824
Subsidies	2 204	2 389	3 491	4 228	4 783	7 808	11 235	10 958	10 272	11 134	11 546
Net national income	42 142	55 167	77 010	104 582	138 250	169 064	202 173	233 800	253 222	251 670	261 218

Source: National Economic Institute.

Table B. Supply and use of resources

IKr Million, constant 1990 prices

	1983	1984	1985	1986	1987	1988	1989	1990	1991	1992	1993
Private consumption	172 514	179 054	186 986	200 543	233 829	223 859	214 553	213 555	224 420	213 936	204 309
Public consumption	50 453	50 706	53 939	57 619	61 394	64 198	66 094	68 854	71 057	70 347	71 754
Gross fixed asset formation	54 515	59 509	60 706	59 981	71 369	70 960	65 085	66 896	68 312	60 661	53 647
Expenditure on final domestic use	277 482	289 269	301 631	318 143	366 592	359 017	345 732	349 305	363 789	344 944	329 710
Change in stocks of export products	-4 051	1 765	-1 887	-4 436	-2 740	1 543	-1 269	-1 797	1 126	34	925
National expenditure	273 431	291 034	299 744	313 707	363 853	360 560	344 462	347 508	364 915	344 978	330 634
Exports of goods and services	102 178	104 737	116 259	123 127	127 762	123 437	126 653	126 456	119 269	117 197	124 348
Imports of goods and services	93 063	101 574	111 141	112 195	138 298	131 957	118 422	119 595	126 239	116 398	106 335
Statistical discrepancy[1]	32	-22	1	46	-145	-132	12	0	0	0	0
Gross domestic product (market prices)	282 578	294 175	304 863	324 685	353 172	351 908	352 705	354 369	357 945	345 777	348 647
Gross national product (market prices)	273 386	283 133	293 415	313 402	341 580	338 186	337 887	339 758	342 620	330 610	332 823
Effect of changes in terms of trade	-2 945	-3 770	-4 918	2 302	8 937	8 098	2 215	2	5 275	2 655	-2 718
Gross national income[2]	270 441	279 363	288 497	315 704	350 517	346 284	340 102	339 760	347 895	333 265	330 105

Note: Estimates of real income coincide with output in real terms on the assumption of unchanged terms of trade. Due to particularly strong fluctuations in Icelandic terms of trade national expenditure in real terms may deviate substantially from real gross national product without adverse effects on the balance of payments. This is explicitly introduced in the Icelandic national accounts, as shown above. The item "Effect of changes in the terms of trade" equals the external purchasing power of export earnings (nominal exports deflated by a price index for imports) minus the volume of exports of goods and services.

1. The presence of a statistical discrepancy in the data prior to 1990 is attributable to the fact that the Icelandic authorities rebased the data without modifying the growth rates in volume terms calculated from the previous 1980 base year data.
2. Gross national product plus effect of changes in terms of trade.

Source: National Economic Institute.

Table C. **Production and employment**

	1983	1984	1985	1986	1987	1988	1989	1990	1991	1992	1993[1]
Fisheries and fish processing											
Output (volume change over previous year)	-9.5	13.8	7.8	10.3	5.0	-0.2	-3.5	-0.6	-3.2	3.3	9.1
Export production Value (IKr million)	12 564	16 562	23 937	32 605	40 220	45 686	55 507	67 952	74 334	70 210	76 752
Fishing fleet[2]:											
Trawlers (GRT)	48 478	50 801	50 844	50 569	51 380	54 086	52 830	49 912	47 493	43 031	41 502[3]
Motor boats (GRT)	63 294	62 046	61 750	61 822	66 072	65 521	63 181	59 366	52 500	47 317	44 747[3]
Total (GRT)	111 772	112 847	112 594	112 391	117 452	119 607	116 011	109 278	99 993	90 348	86 249[3]
Employment (man-years)	16 045	15 802	15 728	16 064	16 788	15 145	14 893	14 746	14 303	13 250	13 000[3]
Agriculture											
Output (volume change over previous year)	1.4	2.7	4.0	-0.4	1.6	-5.0	8.3	-2.1	0.3	-5.9	2.8
Export production Value (IKr million)	237	406	597	690	1 015	997	1 288	1 765	1 657	1 394	1 471[4]
Capacity:											
Cultivated grassland (1 000 hect.)	142.1	143.9	145.1	146.1	146.6	147.0	147.0	146.8	146.5	146.2	145.9
Sheep (1 000 heads)	711.9	714.4	709.3	675.5	624.3	586.9	560.9	548.5	510.8	486.8	487.0
Cattle (1 000 heads)	68.5	72.7	72.9	71.4	69.0	70.8	72.8	74.9	77.7	76.0	74.6
Employment (man-years)	7 864	7 595	7 420	7 374	7 147	6 470	6 399	6 164	6 709	6 400	6 300
Manufacturing (excluding fish processing)											
Output (volume change over previous year)	-1.0	7.4	2.8	2.7	9.3	-5.2	-3.6	-2.9	3.8	-3.6	-4.0
Export production Value (IKr million)	4 528	6 673	7 776	8 794	10 059	13 677	19 460	18 742	15 927	15 132	15 648[4]
of which:											
Aluminium	2 333	3 445	3 472	4 042	4 761	6 705	10 146	9 629	8 222	7 996	7 667[4]
Diatomite	142	189	289	284	296	348	416	522	406	422	374[4]
Ferro-silicon	619	1 060	1 267	1 352	1 195	2 203	2 899	2 180	1 637	1 691	2 449[4]
Employment (man-years)	16 394	16 956	17 620	17 740	18 439	17 057	16 195	15 573	15 583	24 850	14 200

1. Projection.
2. Including whale catchers, excluding open boat.
3. Situation on 1st January, 1994.
4. January to November, 1993.
Source: National Economic Institute and Central Bank of Iceland.

Table D. **Gross fixed asset formation and national wealth**

IKr million, current prices

	1984	1985	1986	1987	1988	1989	1990	1991	1992	1993
Gross fixed asset formation, total	18 356	24 460	29 684	41 042	48 414	56 051	66 896	72 700	66 447	61 300
Classification by end-use:										
Industrial asset formation	7 961	12 230	16 090	22 148	23 959	24 697	29 686	31 300	28 231	21 450
Agriculture	978	1 609	2 226	2 367	2 560	2 448	1 791	1 890	1 698	1 650
Fishing	839	910	2 648	4 192	5 835	3 361	2 361	2 600	5 880	2 100
Fish processing	785	1 137	1 358	1 440	1 509	1 265	1 730	1 410	1 408	1 600
Manufacturing other than fish processing	2 020	3 023	3 457	4 261	4 671	5 865	5 387	6 690	5 432	5 520
Transport equipment	790	1 734	1 403	1 774	1 387	3 846	9 640	9 240	5 209	2 000
Commercial buildings, hotels, etc.	1 269	1 933	2 626	4 770	4 190	4 700	4 721	4 330	4 397	4 130
Various machinery and equipment	1 280	1 884	2 372	3 344	3 807	3 212	4 056	5 140	4 207	4 450
Residential construction	4 714	5 380	5 770	7 752	10 488	13 280	15 555	15 900	15 760	15 000
Public works and buildings	5 681	6 850	7 824	11 142	13 967	18 074	21 655	25 500	22 456	24 850
Electric power, generation and distribution	1 550	991	899	1 177	1 882	3 103	4 881	5 800	2 352	2 200
Geothermal heating and water supply	570	871	840	930	1 650	2 340	1 645	1 450	1 505	1 550
Communications	2 229	3 062	3 625	5 634	5 409	6 288	7 159	9 450	9 829	11 800
Public buildings	1 332	1 926	2 460	3 401	5 026	6 343	7 970	8 800	8 770	9 300
National wealth	264 770	358 439	452 919	550 225	673 496	854 108	1 018 615	1 116 335	1 161 422	
Private sector[1]	81 452	110 275	139 626	167 989	203 437	257 628	311 441	342 653	357 460	
Public works and buildings	95 359	127 827	157 637	192 997	234 900	295 963	367 165	405 671	423 625	
Industrial sector	87 959	120 337	155 656	189 239	235 159	300 517	340 009	368 011	380 337	

1. Residential housing and private automobiles.
Source: National Economic Institute.

Table E. **Gross fixed asset formation and national wealth**

IKr million, constant 1990 prices

	1984	1985	1986	1987	1988	1989	1990	1991	1992	1993
Gross fixed asset formation, total	59 509	60 706	59 981	71 369	70 960	65 085	66 896	68 312	60 661	53 647
Classification by end-use:										
Industrial asset formation	24 572	29 150	31 082	37 489	34 531	27 604	29 686	29 723	25 928	18 288
Agriculture	3 196	4 107	4 709	4 370	3 973	2 964	1 791	1 795	1 590	1 466
Fishing	2 759	2 345	5 264	7 352	8 645	3 892	2 361	2 463	5 408	1 756
Fish processing	2 487	2 734	2 594	2 440	2 146	1 436	1 730	1 336	1 288	1 353
Manufacturing other than fish processing	6 445	7 375	6 702	7 311	6 798	6 734	5 387	6 334	4 976	4 697
Transport equipment	2 374	3 893	2 833	3 277	2 247	4 448	9 640	8 847	4 790	1 689
Commercial buildings, hotels, etc.	3 815	4 394	4 795	7 408	5 523	5 033	4 721	4 020	3 990	3 668
Various machinery and equipment	3 433	4 180	4 169	5 189	5 087	3 263	4 056	4 928	3 886	3 659
Statistical discrepancy[1]	63	122	16	142	112	-166	0	0	0	0
Residential construction	15 603	13 480	11 617	13 267	15 228	15 653	15 555	14 796	14 301	13 322
Public works and buildings	19 519	17 817	16 783	19 970	20 854	21 971	21 655	23 793	20 432	22 037
Electric power, generation and distribution	4 897	2 393	1 748	1 952	2 645	3 558	4 881	5 459	2 140	1 941
Geothermal heating and water supply	1 758	2 064	1 614	1 505	2 266	2 623	1 645	1 348	1 366	1 377
Communications	7 947	8 182	8 182	10 395	8 199	7 779	7 159	8 808	8 968	10 460
Public buildings	4 729	5 167	5 307	6 236	7 830	8 022	7 970	8 178	7 958	8 259
Statistical discrepancy[1]	188	11	-68	-118	-86	-11	0	0	0	0
Statistical discrepancy[1]	-185	259	499	643	347	-143	0	0	0	0
National wealth	893.2	921.0	949.1	995.9	1 034.1	1 071.0	1 079.5	1 105.3	1 114.0	1 123.0
Private sector[2]	304.7	311.8	323.6	343.6	356.7	362.6	368.9	377.3	381.2	382.8
Public works and buildings	327.8	335.5	338.1	345.7	354.1	363.3	371.9	382.6	389.2	397.8
Industrial sector	260.7	273.7	287.4	306.6	323.3	345.1	338.7	345.4	343.6	342.4

1. The presence of statistical discrepancies in the data prior to 1990 is attributable to the fact that the Icelandic authorities rebased the data without modifying the growth rates in volume terms calculated from the previous 1980 base year data.
2. Residential housing and private automobiles.
Source: National Economic Institute.

Table F. **Balance of payments, OECD basis**
US$ million

	1982	1983	1984	1985	1986	1987	1988	1989	1990	1991	1992
Current balance	-263	-57	-131	-115	17	-191	-221	-84	-134	-309	-210
Long term (excl. special transactions)	214	94	113	155	157	178	208	261	278	292	222
a) Private	50	-29	-18	32	47	95	65	70	120	71	-25
b) Official	164	122	131	123	109	83	143	191	159	221	247
Basic balance	-49	37	-18	40	174	-13	-14	177	144	-17	12
Non-monetary short-term private capital	-10	-47	25	128	-43	76	15	-104	-65	48	23
Non-monetary short-term official capital	16	4	23	-58	-4	-16	22	-24	-2	-18	21
Errors and omissions	-47	2	-28	-53	-18	-59	-4	13	-2	20	14
Balance on non-monetary transactions	-90	-5	1	56	108	-12	19	63	75	33	71
Private monetary institutions' short-term capital	-6	16	-16	8	-9	-6	-17	-8	-	-22	10
Balance on official settlements	-95	11	-15	64	99	-18	1	55	74	11	81
Use of IMF credit	18	-1	-	-	-13	-14	-	-	-	-	-
Special transactions	-	-	-	-	-	-	-	-	-	-	-
Miscellaneous official accounts	-	-	-	-	-	-	-	-	-	-	-
Allocations of SDRs	-	-	-	-	-	-	-	-	-	-	-
Change in reserves (+ = increase)	-78	10	-15	64	86	-32	1	55	74	11	81
a) Gold	-	-	-	-	-	-	-	-	-	-	-
b) Currency assets	-66	8	-15	64	87	-34	2	56	74	11	72
c) Reserve position in IMF	-10	4	-	-	-	-	-	-	-	-	9
d) Special Drawing Rights	-2	-2	-	-	-	2	-1	-1	-	-	-

Source: OECD.

Table G. **Central government and social security income and expenditure**

IKr million, accruals basis

	1985	1986	1987	1988	1989	1990	1991	1992	1993[1]
Current revenue	31 304	41 218	53 876	71 300	86 280	95 649	107 935	110 100	109 400
Direct taxes	4 616	7 630	8 273	14 110	17 864	22 565	30 784	31 957	32 214
Indirect taxes	22 850	29 334	40 462	51 011	59 646	65 955	68 792	68 311	68 296
Other	3 838	4 254	5 141	6 179	8 770	7 129	8 359	9 832	8 890
Current expenditure	28 186	36 684	48 318	65 982	81 971	94 094	102 893	105 904	105 870
Public consumption	16 499	22 178	30 387	38 960	46 005	53 728	59 298	59 251	61 643
Interest expenditure	3 300	3 931	4 340	7 174	9 685	11 370	12 962	12 875	12 830
Current transfers and subsidies	8 387	10 575	13 591	19 848	26 281	28 996	30 633	33 778	31 397
Current balance	3 118	4 534	5 558	5 318	4 309	1 555	5 042	4 196	3 530
Capital revenue	680	880	1 234	1 492	1 714	1 976	2 346	2 330	2 420
Capital transfers	129	169	371	474	469	468	610	517	500
Consumption of fixed capital	551	711	863	1 018	1 245	1 508	1 736	1 813	1 920
Capital expenditure	5 812	11 822	8 354	11 824	18 277	15 832	18 398	16 033	16 500
Gross fixed investment	1 888	1 871	3 065	3 961	4 424	6 327	7 095	6 423	7 500
Capital transfers	3 924	9 951	5 289	7 863	13 853	9 505	11 303	9 610	9 000
Capital balance	−5 132	−10 942	−7 120	−10 332	−16 563	−13 856	−16 052	−13 703	−14 080
Financial balance	−2 014	−6 408	−1 562	−5 014	−12 254	−12 301	−11 010	−9 507	−10 550
Net increase in claims	3 225	−3 369	3 782	3 827	680	−924	5 763	−1 761	1 056
Borrowing requirement	5 239	3 039	5 344	8 841	12 934	11 377	16 773	7 746	11 606

1. Preliminary.
Source: National Economic Institute.

Table H. Fish catch, wages and prices

| | Fish catch (thousand metric tons) | | | | | Wages and prices (indices 1980 = 100) | | | | | | | | | |
| | Total | White fish, etc. | Herring | Capelin | Shrimp, lobster, shellfish | Hourly wage rates, unskilled workers[1] | Indices | | | | Export price of fish products[2] | | | |
							Total cost of living	Consumer price index	Credit terms index	Building cost	Fresh and iced fish	Frozen groundfish products	Salted products	Fish meal and oil
1980	1 508	659	53	760	12	100.0	100.0	100.0	100.0	100.0	100.0	100.0	100.0	100.0
1981	1 441	716	40	642	11	152.1	150.9	150.6	151.8	152.4	124.2	144.8	173.3	152.2
1982	788	690	56	13	24	237.2	227.8	227.5	227.4	236.7	220.4	242.9	263.5	191.7
1983	839	603	59	133	31	362.0	419.8	422.6	407.9	403.4	360.0	500.7	448.4	511.6
1984	1 536	565	50	867	42	443.1	542.3	550.7	545.7	505.0	486.2	593.5	519.5	551.4
1985	1 680	586	50	993	44	591.4	717.9	730.5	712.8	668.0	805.0	821.4	726.8	597.8
1986	1 656	632	66	898	55	787.8	870.6	880.9	888.4	832.0	1 048.2	985.0	1 013.8	603.8
1987	1 637	684	75	810	55	1 120.0	1 034.0	1 047.5	1 043.3	979.0	1 180.0	1 163.6	1 295.5	592.7
1988	1 758	697	93	911	42	1 421.0	1 297.2	1 324.5	1 287.2	1 154.0	1 313.9	1 296.2	1 387.7	889.3
1989	1 513	692	97	670	39	1 610.0	1 570.6	1 619.8	1 524.4	1 421.0	1 762.9	1 583.1	1 634.7	1 237.8
1990	1 506	673	90	694	44	1 734.0	1 803.6	1 858.0	1 760.0	1 673.0	2 314.4	2 090.4	2 286.7	1 139.9
1991	1 047	655	78	258	50	1 884.0	1 926.0	1 984.3	1 894.0	1 800.0	2 476.5	2 457.1	2 666.3	1 295.5
1992	1 574	583	123	798	61	1 958.0	1 997.3	2 065.7	1 964.2	1 843.0	2 460.4	2 347.6	2 561.7	1 286.4
1993	1 867	589	107	1 100	63	1 993.0	2 079.0	2 168.2	2 075.0	1 884.0	2 517.6	2 433.9	2 334.4	1 360.1

1. Weighted averages.
2. The index shows the development of export prices (fob) in terms of Icelandic kronur.
Source: National Economic Institute and Central Bank of Iceland, Economic Statistics.

Table I. **Foreign trade, total and by area**

US$ million, monthly rates

	Imports by area							Exports by area						
	Total imports cif	OECD countries				Non-OECD countries		Total exports fob	OECD countries				Non-OECD countries	
		Total	Europe		USA	Eastern Europe	Non-OPEC developing countries		Total	Europe		USA	Eastern Europe	Non-OPEC developing countries
			EEC	Others						EEC	Others			
1978	56.7	47.8	27.4	12.4	4.0	5.6	3.2	54.2	43.6	21.6	5.0	15.9	4.2	3.7
1979	68.8	57.5	34.3	13.9	4.5	8.5	2.7	65.8	58.1	30.7	6.7	18.4	5.3	1.4
1980	83.4	71.0	39.7	15.7	7.8	9.1	3.3	77.5	62.8	36.4	8.1	16.7	6.8	2.2
1981	86.3	74.6	41.0	19.1	6.7	7.8	3.9	75.4	57.3	34.5	5.2	15.7	6.0	1.6
1982	78.6	67.1	38.9	15.6	6.6	7.8	3.7	57.2	48.9	27.8	4.2	14.8	4.8	1.2
1983	69.1	59.5	33.7	14.2	5.4	7.6	2.0	62.5	52.8	27.6	5.5	17.7	5.0	1.6
1984	70.3	60.7	36.2	13.1	4.8	7.5	2.1	61.9	54.6	29.2	5.3	17.6	5.9	1.2
1985	75.5	66.7	40.0	14.9	5.1	6.4	2.3	67.8	61.0	33.1	5.9	18.3	5.3	1.4
1986	93.1	83.9	49.5	19.2	6.5	5.8	3.3	91.2	83.1	49.5	9.2	19.8	5.0	1.5
1987	131.9	119.6	69.1	27.3	9.4	7.2	5.1	114.3	105.4	65.6	9.6	20.9	5.4	1.8
1988	133.6	121.3	69.0	29.7	10.1	7.2	5.1	119.5	108.5	70.6	12.2	16.2	6.3	3.3
1989	116.7	104.5	65.6	22.4	13.0	7.3	4.8	116.7	104.0	65.6	13.3	16.4	6.2	6.0
1990	138.7	124.1	69.5	22.7	19.7	9.0	5.5	132.6	123.2	89.9	11.6	13.1	3.8	4.7
1991	143.0	130.2	75.0	24.6	14.8	5.9	6.8	129.1	123.0	86.3	9.9	16.1	1.1	4.0
1992	140.4	128.3	68.3	35.1	11.6	3.3	8.6	127.3	121.4	87.6	9.3	14.4	0.5	4.3

Source: Central Bank of Iceland, and OECD, *Foreign Trade Statistics*, Series A.

Table J. Foreign trade by commodity group
US$ million

	Imports by commodity group							Exports by commodity group							
	Total	Transport equipment	Other imports					Total	Fish products, total	Frozen fish fillets	Herring salted	Herring and capelin meal	Agricultural products	Aluminium products	Other manufactured products
			Total	Food and live animals	Manufactured goods	Machinery and apparatus	Other goods								
SITC No.		78-79		0	6	71-77									
1979	825.0	74.0	751.0	68.7	159.0	143.7	379.6	789.1	589.3	258.4	22.1	60.9	21.3	106.3	64.3
1980	1 000.1	102.7	897.4	82.3	194.1	172.6	448.4	931.2	697.1	266.4	21.7	61.6	17.7	113.2	88.7
1981	1 021.0	107.8	913.2	81.3	189.4	183.8	458.7	902.5	706.4	237.1	22.1	45.3	13.3	87.5	86.2
1982	941.5	87.5	854.0	76.1	182.3	169.1	426.5	677.0	507.9	220.0	17.7	8.5	9.0	68.0	82.7
1983	815.2	58.4	756.8	72.9	156.7	139.0	388.2	745.3	506.7	245.9	18.3	1.9	9.1	130.9	87.4
1984	821.3	65.4	755.9	69.5	149.6	155.9	380.9	744.2	500.2	222.3	24.5	42.3	13.9	108.2	99.4
1985	904.0	60.7	843.3	72.0	163.1	185.0	423.2	813.9	609.3	261.5	21.2	44.4	13.1	80.5	102.1
1986	1 115.3	135.4	979.9	85.2	211.1	233.3	450.3	1 095.8	843.8	320.7	18.0	57.0	16.9	100.5	115.7
1987	1 581.3	268.4	1 312.9	99.8	275.6	337.9	599.6	1 374.3	1 044.5	381.8	21.7	50.9	26.1	131.6	144.4
1988	1 590.3	266.8	1 323.5	106.7	286.4	318.2	612.2	1 431.2	1 016.9	367.1	24.6	75.1	24.8	153.8	167.0
1989	1 395.0	183.8	1 211.2	110.7	256.6	269.1	574.8	1 401.3	994.3	398.2	21.8	63.1	23.9	180.1	164.8
1990	1 654.6	260.8	1 393.8	122.5	278.4	318.9	674.0	1 587.1	1 197.7	521.9	26.0	53.9	30.5	164.3	159.8
1991	1 738.8	220.7	1 518.1	126.7	309.0	370.7	711.6	1 549.2	1 239.2	589.8	14.8	21.5	27.4	136.6	132.8
1992	1 681.9	246.3	1 435.6	127.4	286.5	331.2	690.6	1 524.3	1 212.8	579.2	11.1	72.8	28.3	139.8	122.7

Source: Central Bank of Iceland and OECD, *Foreign Trade Statistics*, Serie C.

Table K. Money and credit
End of period

| | Central Bank | | Money supply | | | Deposit money banks | | | Credits granted by DMB | | | | | | Foreign exchange | |
	Penalty rates (annual rate)	Net position of government	M1[1]	M2[2]	M3[3]	Required reserves	Demand deposits	Net foreign liquid assets	Total	of which to: Agriculture	Fishery and fish processing	Manufacturing and commerce	Dwellings		Net foreign reserves	Commercial banks' short-term foreign assets
	%[4]								IKr million							
1979	45.0	303	625	1 677	2 503	563	468	47	2 235	378	501	617	273		404	−104
1980	55.8	336	1 010	2 773	4 137	1 003	791	78	3 533	532	817	978	456		910	−323
1981	55.3	268	1 620	4 841	7 056	1 904	1 224	69	6 165	800	1 421	1 645	781		1 637	−447
1982	58.0	145	2 089	7 133	11 149	3 048	1 570	198	11 592	1 273	3 111	3 386	1 197		1 494	−1 217
1983	58.2	852	3 700	12 372	19 902	5 594	2 941	−45	20 628	2 191	5 570	5 806	2 183		2 603	−3 088
1984	31.5	1 159	5 299	18 666	26 575	7 143	4 354	283	30 149	2 860	8 857	8 694	2 830		2 160	−5 710
1985	44.0	3 147	6 662	30 126	39 135	7 987	5 436	144	39 622	4 028	8 537	12 567	3 678		7 671	−10 022
1986	30.5	2 806	9 682	41 368	52 940	10 778	7 991	461	48 651	4 972	7 602	15 782	4 651		11 273	−7 860
1987	35.9	5 550	12 750	56 902	71 602	11 159	10 562	658	71 701	6 367	11 699	22 596	6 171		10 536	−11 105
1988	43.9	9 117	14 853	73 271	88 802	12 162	12 302	1 700	95 504	7 681	17 161	28 737	8 064		11 919	−15 399
1989	35.9	8 237	19 725	92 548	112 998	14 711	16 750	2 943	118 130	9 254	19 261	34 518	11 325		20 005	−11 512
1990	26.0	3 594	24 644	105 731	129 802	11 223	21 587	2 379	136 539	10 589	17 939	36 037	12 916		23 412	−8 596
1991	25.0	8 748	29 553	116 697	148 436	10 418	26 314	3 506	152 927	10 768	19 307	40 854	14 051		24 066	−10 008
1992	19.5	1 551	29 942	116 801	154 101	9 255	26 350	3 413	159 642	8 887	19 568	41 964	14 771		31 053	−12 898
1993		5 774	31 620	117 374	163 674	7 186	27 728	5 848	172 923	8 222	20 218	41 143	14 389		28 659	−9 288

1. Notes and coins, demand deposits.
2. Broad money, *i.e.* M1 plus general savings deposits.
3. M2 plus time deposits.
4. Annual average.
Source: Central Bank of Iceland.

108

Table L. **Public sector**

	1960	1970	1980	1989	1990	1991	1992	1993
General government accounts (as a per cent of GDP)								
Current revenue	28.2	30.2	33.1	34.9	34.0	35.1	35.6	35.0
Tax revenue[1]	27.2	29.6	30.9	32.1	31.5	32.5	33.0	31.7
Interest income	..	..	1.9	2.2	1.6	1.8	1.5	1.5
Capital revenue	..	..	0.2	0.7	0.7	0.8	0.8	0.9
Total expenses	25.8	29.9	32.4	39.5	37.5	38.6	39.2	39.6
of which:								
Current expenditure	..	..	26.0	31.9	31.5	32.1	33.4	33.6
Current transfers	..	..	4.3	5.4	5.3	5.6	6.0	6.3
Subsidies	..	..	3.1	3.6	3.1	2.7	3.0	2.3
Capital expenditure	..	..	6.4	8.3	6.7	7.2	6.6	6.0
Gross fixed investment	..	..	3.7	4.1	4.1	4.2	4.0	4.1
Capital transfers	..	..	2.7	4.2	2.6	3.0	2.6	2.0
Tax receipts as a per cent of general government total taxes								
General government								
Direct taxes	31.5	30.9	26.9	30.2	32.4	36.2	36.9	40.4
Indirect taxes	68.5	69.1	73.1	69.8	67.6	63.8	63.1	59.6
Central government and Social security								
Total taxes	77.5	77.2	79.8	78.2	79.1	78.9	78.2	78.2
Direct taxes	13.3	16.8	15.9	18.0	20.1	24.2	24.4	24.1
Indirect taxes	64.2	60.4	63.9	60.2	59.0	54.7	53.8	54.2
Local government								
Total taxes	22.5	22.8	20.2	21.8	20.9	21.1	21.8	21.8
Direct taxes	18.2	14.1	11.0	12.2	12.3	12.0	12.5	16.3
Indirect taxes	4.3	8.7	9.2	9.6	8.6	9.1	9.2	5.5

1. Direct and indirect taxes.
Source: National Economic Institute et Sögulegt Yfirlit Hagtalna, 1945-1988, National Economic Institute.

Table M. **Labour market**

	Capital area	Western Iceland	West Fjords	North west Iceland	North east Iceland	Eastern Iceland	Southern Iceland	Reykjanes peninsula	Total
Employment (number of man years)									
1980	57 481	6 510	5 208	4 674	11 104	5 913	8 602	6 783	106 275
1988	76 858	7 133	5 190	4 950	12 105	5 978	9 057	7 471	128 742
1990	72 970	6 965	5 327	4 989	11 867	5 758	9 401	7 462	124 739
1991	72 828	6 980	5 304	4 968	11 860	5 759	9 388	7 390	124 477
1992	72 254	6 966	5 328	4 969	11 834	5 762	9 338	7 200	123 650
1993	71 296	6 936	5 276	4 957	11 677	5 722	9 290	7 248	122 402
Unemployment rate (per cent)									
1980	0.2	0.2	0.1	0.9	0.7	0.5	0.4	0.3	0.3
1988	0.2	1.4	0.3	2.0	1.4	1.2	1.5	0.7	0.6
1990	1.2	2.6	0.4	3.0	3.3	3.3	2.4	1.9	1.8
1991	0.9	1.9	0.3	2.9	2.8	2.8	2.1	2.3	1.5
1992	2.6	3.0	0.8	3.7	3.9	3.6	3.5	5.6	3.0
1993	4.2	3.7	2.2	4.3	5.6	4.6	4.4	5.4	4.3

	1961	1970	1980	1988	1989	1990	1991	1992
Population by age group (per cent change over previous year)								
Under 15 and over 65 years	2.0	-0.4	0.3	0.6	0.8	0.8	1.1	1.1
Between 15 and 19 years	3.3	1.8	-0.4	1.4	0.9	1.5	1.0	-1.1
Between 20 and 64 years	1.9	1.1	1.9	1.1	1.4	0.8	1.4	1.4
Between 15 and 64 years	2.1	1.2	1.5	1.1	1.3	0.8	1.2	1.0
Total population	2.1	0.5	1.1	1.6	2.1	0.8	1.3	1.1
Labour supply (per cent change over previous year)	-0.1	2.0	3.3	-2.8	-0.4	-0.9	-0.5	0.9
Work stoppages								
Number of stoppages	..	65	14	15	16	1	7	4
Working days lost	..	48	48	131	611	31	27	6
Number of participants	..	15 705	4 220	11 642	2 028	177	751	611
Number of man-days lost	..	303 743	30 760	100 773	79 970	231	3 413	385
Non-seamen in ASI	..	296 596	16 044	110 773	2 250	231	1 873	32
Seamen	..	7 147	3 696	0	0	0	1 540	0
Others	..	0	11 020	0	77 720	0	0	353

Source: National Economic Institute.

BASIC STATISTICS

BASIC STATISTICS:

INTERNATIONAL COMPARISONS

	Units	Reference period [1]	Australia	Austri
Population				
Total	Thousands	1991	17 292	7 823
Inhabitants per sq. km	Number	1991	2	93
Net average annual increase over previous 10 years	%	1991	1.5	0.3
Employment				
Total civilian employment (TCE) [2]	Thousands	1991	7 705	3 482
Of which: Agriculture	% of TCE		5.5	7.4
Industry	% of TCE		24.2	36.9
Services	% of TCE		70.4	55.8
Gross domestic product (GDP)				
At current prices and current exchange rates	Bill. US$	1991	297.4	164.7
Per capita	US$		17 200	21 048
At current prices using current PPP's [3]	Bill. US$	1991	280	135.6
Per capita	US$		16 195	17 329
Average annual volume growth over previous 5 years	%	1991	2.8	3.3
Gross fixed capital formation (GFCF)	% of GDP	1991	20.5	25.1
Of which: Machinery and equipment	% of GDP		8.8	10.4
Residential construction	% of GDP		4.6	4.6
Average annual volume growth over previous 5 years	%	1991	0.3	5.2
Gross saving ratio [4]	% of GDP	1991	17.2	25.6
General government				
Current expenditure on goods and services	% of GDP	1991	18.3	18.2
Current disbursements [5]	% of GDP	1991	36.6	45.7
Current receipts	% of GDP	1991	33.7	47.2
Net official development assistance	% of GDP	1991	0.35	0.33
Indicators of living standards				
Private consumption per capita using current PPP's [3]	US$	1991	9 827	9 591
Passenger cars, per 1 000 inhabitants	Number	1990	430	382
Telephones, per 1 000 inhabitants	Number	1990	448 (89)	589
Television sets, per 1 000 inhabitants	Number	1989	484	475
Doctors, per 1 000 inhabitants	Number	1991	2	2.1
Infant mortality per 1 000 live births	Number	1991	7.1	7.4
Wages and prices (average annual increase over previous 5 years)				
Wages (earnings or rates according to availability)	%	1991	5.4	5.2
Consumer prices	%	1991	6.7	2.5
Foreign trade				
Exports of goods, fob*	Mill. US$	1991	39 764	40 985
As % of GDP	%		13.4	24.9
Average annual increase over previous 5 years	%		13.2	12.8
Imports of goods, cif*	Mill. US$	1991	38 844	48 914
As % of GDP	%		13.1	29.7
Average annual increase over previous 5 years	%		10.1	13.7
Total official reserves [6]	Mill. SDR's	1991	11 432	6 591
As ratio of average monthly imports of goods	Ratio		3.5	1.6

* At current prices and exchange rates.
1. Unless otherwise stated.
2. According to the definitions used in OECD *Labour Force Statistics*.
3. PPP's = Purchasing Power Parities.
4. Gross saving = Gross national disposable income minus private and government consumption.
5. Current disbursements = Current expenditure on goods and services plus current transfers and payments of property income.
6. Gold included in reserves is valued at 35 SDR's per ounce. End of year.
7. Including Luxembourg.

Belgium	Canada	Denmark	Finland	France	Germany	Greece	Iceland	Irelan
0 005	27 000	5 154	5 029	57 050	63 889	10 269	258	3 524
328	3	120	15	104	257	78	3	50
0.2	1	0.1	0.5	0.5	0.4	0.5	1.1	0.2
3 735	12 340	2 612	2 330	21 782	28 533	3 768	140	1 113
2.6	4.5	5.7	8.5	5.8	3.4	22.6	10.7	13.8
28.1	23.2	27.7	29.2	29.5	39.2	27.5	26.4	28.9
69.3	72.3	66.6	62.3	64.8	57.4	50	62.9	57.2
196.9	583.7	130.3	121.2	1 195.8	1 587.8	70.2	6.5	43.4
9 677	21 617	25 277	24 097	20 961	24 852	6 840	25 232	12 324
171.5	520.6	90.7	77.8	1 035.6	1 257.8	79.4	4.5	40.5
7 145	19 281	17 603	15 480	18 152	19 687	7 729	17 442	11 480
3.2	1.9	1.1	1.4	2.7	3.8	1.9	2	5.4
19.8	20	16.9	22.4	20.9	21.4	18.6	18.9	17.1
10.4 (90)	6.4	8.5	7.4	9.4	10	7.8	6	7.7
4.2	6.2	3.2	6.1	5.1	5.7	4.4	4.1	4.1
8.5	4.2	−2.9	0.1	4.6	5.4	3.5	2.6	3
21.4	14.4	17.9	14.7	20.7	23.1	15.3	14.4	23.7
14.7	21.3	25.1	24.4	18.3	17.7	19.9	20	16.3
54.6	47.9	57.2	46	47	44.2	47.6	32.5	49.9
49.8	43.1	55.5	42.6	46.5	44.5	37	35.1	43.7
0.42	0.45	0.92	0.77	0.62	0.43	0.08	0.12	0.17
0 756	11 634	9 139	8 686	10 928	10 672	5 516	10 731	6 409
387	469	311	386	413	480	169	464	228
546	570	972	530	482	671	458	496	279
447	626	528	488	400	506	195	319	271
3.6	2.2	2.8	2.5	2.7	3.2	3.4	2.8	1.5
8.4	6.8	7.5	5.8	7.3	7.1	9	5.5	8.2
3.5	4.5	5.9	8.3	3.8	4.7	16.9	. .	5.3
2.5	4.8	3.7	5.2	3.2	2.1	16.7	17.2	3.2
8 291 [7]	127 658	34 988	26 508	216 157	409 620	8 014	1 589	23 796
60.1	21.9	26.9	21.9	18.1	25.8	11.4	24.4	54.8
11.4	7.9	11.1	7.1	11.7	10.6	8.9	8.1	14
0 330 [7]	116 729	31 647	26 953	225 260	344 454	19 831	1 655	20 687
61.1	20	24.3	22.2	18.8	21.7	28.2	25.4	47.6
12	7.8	7.2	7.2	12.2	15.3	11.9	9	12.4
8 541 [7]	12 544	7 445	6 779	25 851	47 729	2 398	307	3 672
0.9	1.3	2.8	3	1.4	1.7	1.5	2.2	2.1

8.   Included
9.   Including
Sources: Pop
          GDP, GF
          Indicators
          Wages a
          Foreign
          Total offi

	Italy	Japan	Luxembourg	Netherlands	New Zealand	Norway	Portug
	57 114	123 920	390	15 070	3 406	4 262	9 814
	190	328	150	369	13	13	106
	0.1	0.5	0.6	0.6	0.8	0.4	0
	21 410	63 690	162	6 444	1 451	1 973	4 607
	8.5	6.7	3.7	4.5	10.8	5.9	17.3
	32.3	34.4	31.5	25.5	23.5	23.7	33.9
	59.2	58.9	64.8	69.9	65.7	70.4	48.7
	1 149.9	3 346.4	9.3	289.8	42.2	105.9	68.6
	19 900	27 005	24 186	19 232	12 400	24 853	6 991
	974.6	2 349.2	8.1	248	46.6	71.6	90.1
	16 866	18 957	20 904	16 453	13 675	16 804	9 180
	2.7	4.8	4.3	2.9	−0.2	1.1	4.2
	19.8	31.7	29	20.5	16.4	18.5	26
	9.4	13.1	12.4	10	9.9 (90)	11.7 (87)	7.6
	5.3	5.5	5.5	4.7	4.8 (90)	2.1	4.5
	4.1	8.5	9.9	2.5	−1.3	−6.6	8.7
	18.6	35.1	59.4	24.7	15	23.6	25.4
	17.5	9.2	17.1	14.4	16.6	21.5	17.8
(87)	49.4	25.4	45 (86)	54.8	. .	52.9	39.3
(87)	43	34.4	52.9 (86)	54.6	. .	55.3	37.6
	0.29	0.33	0.42	0.87	0.24	1.1	0.31
	10 418	10 738	11 973	9 807	8 771	8 558	5 810
	478	282	470	356 (89)	440	378	260
	555	421	413	462	430	502	263
	423	610	252	485	372	423	176
	1.3	1.6	2.1	2.5	1.9	3.1	2.8
	8.3	4.6	9.2	6.5	8.3	7	10.8
	7.1	4.1	. .	2.2	5.2	7.6	. .
	5.7	1.9	2.3	1.5	7.2	5.5	11.3
	170 258	286 314	8	131 361	9 515	33 808	16 338
	14.8	8.6	. .	45.3	22.5	31.9	23.8
	11.6	8.5	. .	10.6	10.5	13.1	17.4
	181 925	233 814	. .	126 158	9 464	27 164	24 874
	15.8	7	. .	43.5	22.4	25.6	36.3
	12.8	13.1	. .	10.9	6.8	4.6	22.6
	44 232	55 179	. .	12 289	2 902	10 777	10 182
	2.9	2.8	. .	1.2	3.7	4.8	4.9

Belgium.
on-residential construction.
lation and employment: OECD, *Labour Force Statistics*.
F, and general government: OECD, *National Accounts*, Vol. 1 and *OECD Economic Outlook*, Historical Statistics.
of living standards: miscellaneous national publications.
prices: OECD, *Main Economic Indicators*.
le: OECD, *Monthly Foreign Trade Statistics*, series A.
al reserves: IMF, *International Financial Statistics*.

	Spain	Sweden	Switzerland	Turkey	United Kingdom	United States
	39 025	8 617	6 792	57 693	57 649	252 160
	77	19	165	74	236	27
	0.3	0.3	0.6	2.3	0.2	0.9
	12 608	4 431	3 560	18 171	25 726	116 877
	10.7	3.2	5.5	46.6	2.2	2.9
	33.1	28.2	34.4	20.3	27.8	25.3
	56.3	68.5	60.1	33.1	70	71.8
	527.6	239.3	230.9	108	1 008.4	5 610.8
	13 519	27 774	33 992	1 872	17 492	22 204
	496.2	145.4	148.3	201.1	899.8	5 610.8
	12 714	16 877	21 832	3 486	15 608	22 204
	4.3	1.6	2.2	4.7	2	1.9
	23.9	19.4	25.6	22.8	16.9	15.4
	7.1					
(90)	4.7	6.2	16.9[9]	5.8 (87)	3	3.4
	9.9	3.3	4	3.1	2.8	−0.5
	21	16	31.6	21.2	13.5	15
	16.1	27.2	13.9	22.5	21.7	18.2
(90)	35.5 (88)	59.8	32.5	..	39.7	36.7
(90)	36.3 (88)	60	34.2	..	38.8	32.5
	0.22	0.88	0.37	..	0.32	0.2
	7 935	8 994	12 607	1995	9 912	14 891
	307	418	441	29	361	568
	323	681	905	151	434	509
	389	471	406	174	434	814
	3.9	2.9	3	0.9	1.4	2.3
	7.8	6.1	6.2	56.5	7.4	8.9
	7.6	7.7	..	..	8.6	2.8
	5.9	7.2	3.5	60.3	6.4	4.4
	55 353	57 422	63 893	13 057	184 087	393 812
	10.5	24	27.7	12.1	18.3	7
	17.1	8.1	10.2	12.9	11.5	13.2
	87 449	54 659	69 863	22 566	222 522	494 842
	16.6	22.8	30.3	20.9	22.1	8.8
	21.6	8.8	10	13.5	10.7	6
	36 008	12 644	20 541	4 252	25 201	50 791
	4.9	2.8	3.5	2.3	1.4	1.2

EMPLOYMENT OPPORTUNITIES

Economics Department, OECD

The Economics Department of the OECD offers challenging and rewarding opportunities to economists interested in applied policy analysis in an international environment. The Department's concerns extend across the entire field of economic policy analysis, both macro-economic and micro-economic. Its main task is to provide, for discussion by committees of senior officials from Member countries, documents and papers dealing with current policy concerns. Within this programme of work, three major responsibilities are:

- to prepare regular surveys of the economies of individual Member countries;
- to issue full twice-yearly reviews of the economic situation and prospects of the OECD countries in the context of world economic trends;
- to analyse specific policy issues in a medium-term context for theOECD as a whole, and to a lesser extent for the non-OECD countries.

The documents prepared for these purposes, together with much of the Department's other economic work, appear in published form in the *OECD Economic Outlook, OECD Economic Surveys, OECD Economic Studies* and the Department's *Working Papers* series.

The Department maintains a world econometric model, INTERLINK, which plays an important role in the preparation of the policy analyses and twice-yearly projections. The availability of extensive cross-country data bases and good computer resources facilitates comparative empirical analysis, much of which is incorporated into the model.

The Department is made up of about 75 professional economists from a variety of backgrounds and Member countries. Most projects are carried out by small teams and last from four to eighteen months. Within the Department, ideas and points of view are widely discussed; there is a lively professional interchange, and all professional staff have the opportunity to contribute actively to the programme of work.

Skills the Economics Department is looking for:

a) Solid competence in using the tools of both micro-economic and macro-economic theory to answer policy questions. Experience indicates that this normally requires the equivalent of a PH.D. in economics or substantial relevant professional experience to compensate for a lower degree.

b) Solid knowledge of economic statistics and quantitative methods; this includes how to identify data, estimate structural relationships, apply basic techniques of time series analysis, and test hypotheses. It is essential to be able to interpret results sensibly in an economic policy context.

c) A keen interest in and knowledge of policy issues, economic developments and their political/social contexts.

d) Interest and experience in analysing questions posed by policy-makers and presenting the results to them effectively and judiciously. Thus, work experience in government agencies or policy research institutions is an advantage.

e) The ability to write clearly, effectively, and to the point. The OECD is a bilingual organisation with French and English as the official languages. Candidates must have excellent knowledge of one of these languages, and some knowledge of the other. Knowledge of other languages might also be an advantage for certain posts.

f) For some posts, expertise in a particular area may be important, but a successful candidate is expected to be able to work on a broader range of topics relevant to the work of the Department. Thus, except in rare cases, the Department does not recruit narrow specialists.

g) The Department works on a tight time schedule and strict deadlines. Moreover, much of the work in the Department is carried out in small groups of economists. Thus, the ability to work with other economists from a variety of cultural and professional backgrounds, to supervise junior staff, and to produce work on time is important.

General Information

The salary for recruits depends on educational and professional background. Positions carry a basic salary from FF 262 512 or FF 323 916 for Administrators (economists) and from FF 375 708 for Principal Administrators (senior economists). This may be supplemented by expatriation and/or family allowances, depending on nationality, residence and family situation. Initial appointments are for a fixed term of two to three years.

Vacancies are open to candidates from OECD Member countries. The Organisation seeks to maintain an appropriate balance between female and male staff and among nationals from Member countries.

For further information on employment opportunities in the Economics Department, contact:

Administrative Unit
Economics Department
OECD
2, rue André-Pascal
75775 PARIS CEDEX 16
FRANCE

Applications citing ''ECSUR'', together with a detailed *curriculum vitae* in English or French, should be sent to the Head of Personnel at the above address.

MAIN SALES OUTLETS OF OECD PUBLICATIONS
PRINCIPAUX POINTS DE VENTE DES PUBLICATIONS DE L'OCDE

ARGENTINA – ARGENTINE
Carlos Hirsch S.R.L.
Galería Güemes, Florida 165, 4° Piso
1333 Buenos Aires   Tel. (1) 331.1787 y 331.2391
Telefax: (1) 331.1787

AUSTRALIA – AUSTRALIE
D.A. Information Services
648 Whitehorse Road, P.O.B 163
Mitcham, Victoria 3132   Tel. (03) 873.4411
Telefax: (03) 873.5679

AUSTRIA – AUTRICHE
Gerold & Co.
Graben 31
Wien I   Tel. (0222) 533.50.14

BELGIUM – BELGIQUE
Jean De Lannoy
Avenue du Roi 202
B-1060 Bruxelles   Tel. (02) 538.51.69/538.08.41
Telefax: (02) 538.08.41

CANADA
Renouf Publishing Company Ltd.
1294 Algoma Road
Ottawa, ON K1B 3W8   Tel. (613) 741.4333
Telefax: (613) 741.5439
Stores:
61 Sparks Street
Ottawa, ON K1P 5R1   Tel. (613) 238.8985
211 Yonge Street
Toronto, ON M5B 1M4   Tel. (416) 363.3171
Telefax: (416)363.59.63
Les Éditions La Liberté Inc.
3020 Chemin Sainte-Foy
Sainte-Foy, PQ G1X 3V6   Tel. (418) 658.3763
Telefax: (418) 658.3763

Federal Publications Inc.
165 University Avenue, Suite 701
Toronto, ON M5H 3B8   Tel. (416) 860.1611
Telefax: (416) 860.1608
Les Publications Fédérales
1185 Université
Montréal, QC H3B 3A7   Tel. (514) 954.1633
Telefax : (514) 954.1635

CHINA – CHINE
China National Publications Import
Export Corporation (CNPIEC)
16 Gongti E. Road, Chaoyang District
P.O. Box 88 or 50
Beijing 100704 PR   Tel. (01) 506.6688
Telefax: (01) 506.3101

DENMARK – DANEMARK
Munksgaard Book and Subscription Service
35, Nørre Søgade, P.O. Box 2148
DK-1016 København K   Tel. (33) 12.85.70
Telefax: (33) 12.93.87

FINLAND – FINLANDE
Akateeminen Kirjakauppa
Keskuskatu 1, P.O. Box 128
00100 Helsinki
Subscription Services/Agence d'abonnements :
P.O. Box 23
00371 Helsinki   Tel. (358 0) 12141
Telefax: (358 0) 121.4450

FRANCE
OECD/OCDE
Mail Orders/Commandes par correspondance:
2, rue André-Pascal
75775 Paris Cedex 16   Tel. (33-1) 45.24.82.00
Telefax: (33-1) 49.10.42.76
Telex: 640048 OCDE

OECD Bookshop/Librairie de l'OCDE :
33, rue Octave-Feuillet
75016 Paris   Tel. (33-1) 45.24.81.67
(33-1) 45.24.81.81
Documentation Française
29, quai Voltaire
75007 Paris   Tel. 40.15.70.00
Gibert Jeune (Droit-Économie)
6, place Saint-Michel
75006 Paris   Tel. 43.25.91.19
Librairie du Commerce International
10, avenue d'Iéna
75016 Paris   Tel. 40.73.34.60
Librairie Dunod
Université Paris-Dauphine
Place du Maréchal de Lattre de Tassigny
75016 Paris   Tel. (1) 44.05.40.13
Librairie Lavoisier
11, rue Lavoisier
75008 Paris   Tel. 42.65.39.95
Librairie L.G.D.J. - Montchrestien
20, rue Soufflot
75005 Paris   Tel. 46.33.89.85
Librairie des Sciences Politiques
30, rue Saint-Guillaume
75007 Paris   Tel. 45.48.36.02
P.U.F.
49, boulevard Saint-Michel
75005 Paris   Tel. 43.25.83.40
Librairie de l'Université
12a, rue Nazareth
13100 Aix-en-Provence   Tel. (16) 42.26.18.08
Documentation Française
165, rue Garibaldi
69003 Lyon   Tel. (16) 78.63.32.23
Librairie Decitre
29, place Bellecour
69002 Lyon   Tel. (16) 72.40.54.54

GERMANY – ALLEMAGNE
OECD Publications and Information Centre
August-Bebel-Allee 6
D-53175 Bonn 2   Tel. (0228) 959.120
Telefax: (0228) 959.12.17

GREECE – GRÈCE
Librairie Kauffmann
Mavrokordatou 9
106 78 Athens   Tel. (01) 32.55.321
Telefax: (01) 36.33.967

HONG-KONG
Swindon Book Co. Ltd.
13–15 Lock Road
Kowloon, Hong Kong   Tel. 366.80.31
Telefax: 739.49.75

HUNGARY – HONGRIE
Euro Info Service
POB 1271
1464 Budapest   Tel. (1) 111.62.16
Telefax : (1) 111.60.61

ICELAND – ISLANDE
Mál Mog Menning
Laugavegi 18, Pósthólf 392
121 Reykjavik   Tel. 162.35.23

INDIA – INDE
Oxford Book and Stationery Co.
Scindia House
New Delhi 110001   Tel.(11) 331.5896/5308
Telefax: (11) 332.5993
17 Park Street
Calcutta 700016   Tel. 240832

INDONESIA – INDONÉSIE
Pdii-Lipi
P.O. Box 269/JKSMG/88
Jakarta 12790   Tel. 583467
Telex: 62 875

IRELAND – IRLANDE
TDC Publishers – Library Suppliers
12 North Frederick Street
Dublin 1   Tel. (01) 874.48.35
Telefax: (01) 874.84.16

ISRAEL
Electronic Publications only
Publications électroniques seulement
Praedicta
5 Shatna Street
P.O. Box 34030
Jerusalem 91340   Tel. (2) 52.84.90/1/2
Telefax: (2) 52.84.93

ITALY – ITALIE
Libreria Commissionaria Sansoni
Via Duca di Calabria 1/1
50125 Firenze   Tel. (055) 64.54.15
Telefax: (055) 64.12.57
Via Bartolini 29
20155 Milano   Tel. (02) 36.50.83
Editrice e Libreria Herder
Piazza Montecitorio 120
00186 Roma   Tel. 679.46.28
Telefax: 678.47.51
Libreria Hoepli
Via Hoepli 5
20121 Milano   Tel. (02) 86.54.46
Telefax: (02) 805.28.86
Libreria Scientifica
Dott. Lucio de Biasio 'Aeiou'
Via Coronelli, 6
20146 Milano   Tel. (02) 48.95.45.52
Telefax: (02) 48.95.45.48

JAPAN – JAPON
OECD Publications and Information Centre
Landic Akasaka Building
2-3-4 Akasaka, Minato-ku
Tokyo 107   Tel. (81.3) 3586.2016
Telefax: (81.3) 3584.7929

KOREA – CORÉE
Kyobo Book Centre Co. Ltd.
P.O. Box 1658, Kwang Hwa Moon
Seoul   Tel. 730.78.91
Telefax: 735.00.30

MALAYSIA – MALAISIE
Co-operative Bookshop Ltd.
University of Malaya
P.O. Box 1127, Jalan Pantai Baru
59700 Kuala Lumpur
Malaysia   Tel. 756.5000/756.5425
Telefax: 757.3661

MEXICO – MEXIQUE
Revistas y Periodicos Internacionales S.A. de C.V.
Florencia 57 - 1004
Mexico, D.F. 06600   Tel. 207.81.00
Telefax : 208.39.79

NETHERLANDS – PAYS-BAS
SDU Uitgeverij Plantijnstraat
Externe Fondsen
Postbus 20014
2500 EA 's-Gravenhage   Tel. (070) 37.89.880
Voor bestellingen: Telefax: (070) 34.75.778

NEW ZEALAND
NOUVELLE-ZÉLANDE
Legislation Services
P.O. Box 12418
Thorndon, Wellington   Tel. (04) 496.5652
                              Telefax: (04) 496.5698

NORWAY – NORVÈGE
Narvesen Info Center – NIC
Bertrand Narvesens vei 2
P.O. Box 6125 Etterstad
0602 Oslo 6   Tel. (022) 57.33.00
                              Telefax: (022) 68.19.01

PAKISTAN
Mirza Book Agency
65 Shahrah Quaid-E-Azam
Lahore 54000   Tel. (42) 353.601
                              Telefax: (42) 231.730

PHILIPPINE – PHILIPPINES
International Book Center
5th Floor, Filipinas Life Bldg.
Ayala Avenue
Metro Manila   Tel. 81.96.76
                              Telex 23312 RHP PH

PORTUGAL
Livraria Portugal
Rua do Carmo 70-74
Apart. 2681
1200 Lisboa   Tel.: (01) 347.49.82/5
                              Telefax: (01) 347.02.64

SINGAPORE – SINGAPOUR
Gower Asia Pacific Pte Ltd.
Golden Wheel Building
41, Kallang Pudding Road, No. 04-03
Singapore 1334   Tel. 741.5166
                              Telefax: 742.9356

SPAIN – ESPAGNE
Mundi-Prensa Libros S.A.
Castelló 37, Apartado 1223
Madrid 28001   Tel. (91) 431.33.99
                              Telefax: (91) 575.39.98

Libreria Internacional AEDOS
Consejo de Ciento 391
08009 – Barcelona   Tel. (93) 488.30.09
                              Telefax: (93) 487.76.59
Llibreria de la Generalitat
Palau Moja
Rambla dels Estudis, 118
08002 – Barcelona
              (Subscripcions) Tel. (93) 318.80.12
              (Publicacions) Tel. (93) 302.67.23
                              Telefax: (93) 412.18.54

SRI LANKA
Centre for Policy Research
c/o Colombo Agencies Ltd.
No. 300-304, Galle Road
Colombo 3   Tel. (1) 574240, 573551-2
                   Telefax: (1) 575394, 510711

SWEDEN – SUÈDE
Fritzes Information Center
Box 16356
Regeringsgatan 12
106 47 Stockholm   Tel. (08) 690.90.90
                              Telefax: (08) 20.50.21
Subscription Agency/Agence d'abonnements :
Wennergren-Williams Info AB
P.O. Box 1305
171 25 Solna   Tel. (08) 705.97.50
                              Téléfax : (08) 27.00.71

SWITZERLAND – SUISSE
Maditec S.A. (Books and Periodicals - Livres
et périodiques)
Chemin des Palettes 4
Case postale 266
1020 Renens   Tel. (021) 635.08.65
                              Telefax: (021) 635.07.80

Librairie Payot S.A.
4, place Pépinet
CP 3212
1002 Lausanne   Tel. (021) 341.33.48
                              Telefax: (021) 341.33.45

Librairie Unilivres
6, rue de Candolle
1205 Genève   Tel. (022) 320.26.23
                              Telefax: (022) 329.73.18

Subscription Agency/Agence d'abonnements :
Dynapresse Marketing S.A.
38 avenue Vibert
1227 Carouge   Tel.: (022) 308.07.89
                              Telefax : (022) 308.07.99

See also – Voir aussi :
OECD Publications and Information Centre
August-Bebel-Allee 6
D-53175 Bonn 2 (Germany) Tel. (0228) 959.120
                              Telefax: (0228) 959.12.17

TAIWAN – FORMOSE
Good Faith Worldwide Int'l. Co. Ltd.
9th Floor, No. 118, Sec. 2
Chung Hsiao E. Road
Taipei   Tel. (02) 391.7396/391.7397
                              Telefax: (02) 394.9176

THAILAND – THAÏLANDE
Suksit Siam Co. Ltd.
113, 115 Fuang Nakhon Rd.
Opp. Wat Rajbopith
Bangkok 10200   Tel. (662) 225.9531/2
                              Telefax: (662) 222.5188

TURKEY – TURQUIE
Kültür Yayinlari Is-Türk Ltd. Sti.
Atatürk Bulvari No. 191/Kat 13
Kavaklidere/Ankara   Tel. 428.11.40 Ext. 2458
Dolmabahce Cad. No. 29
Besiktas/Istanbul   Tel. 260.71.88
                              Telex: 43482B

UNITED KINGDOM – ROYAUME-UNI
HMSO
Gen. enquiries   Tel. (071) 873 0011
Postal orders only:
P.O. Box 276, London SW8 5DT
Personal Callers HMSO Bookshop
49 High Holborn, London WC1V 6HB
                              Telefax: (071) 873 8200
Branches at: Belfast, Birmingham, Bristol, Edin-
burgh, Manchester

UNITED STATES – ÉTATS-UNIS
OECD Publications and Information Centre
2001 L Street N.W., Suite 700
Washington, D.C. 20036-4910 Tel. (202) 785.6323
                              Telefax: (202) 785.0350

VENEZUELA
Libreria del Este
Avda F. Miranda 52, Aptdo. 60337
Edificio Galipán
Caracas 106   Tel. 951.1705/951.2307/951.1297
                      Telegram: Libreste Caracas

Subscription to OECD periodicals may also be
placed through main subscription agencies.

Les abonnements aux publications périodiques de
l'OCDE peuvent être souscrits auprès des
principales agences d'abonnement.

Orders and inquiries from countries where Distribu-
tors have not yet been appointed should be sent to:
OECD Publications Service, 2 rue André-Pascal,
75775 Paris Cedex 16, France.

Les commandes provenant de pays où l'OCDE n'a
pas encore désigné de distributeur devraient être
adressées à : OCDE, Service des Publications,
2, rue André-Pascal, 75775 Paris Cedex 16, France.

3-1994

PRINTED IN FRANCE

•

OECD PUBLICATIONS
2 rue André-Pascal
75775 PARIS CEDEX 16
No. 47203
(10 94 17 1) ISBN 92-64-14127-8
ISSN 0376-6438

•